The Book of
Tree Spells

CHERALYN DARCEY

ROCKPOOL

For my brother Glenn,
the forest-keeper, the magic and magick maker,
the off-the-grid farmer and musician.
Your legacy of inspiration, like the trees,
will grow forever.

❦

Until you dig a hole, you plant a tree, you water it and make it survive,
you haven't done a thing. You are just talking.
Wangari Maathai

❧

A Rockpool book
PO Box 252
Summer Hill, NSW 2130
Australia
rockpoolpublishing.com

First published in 2019

ISBN 978-1-925682-88-5

A catalogue record for this book is available from the
National Library of Australia.

Cover design by Richard Crookes
Internal design by Jessica Le, Rockpool Publishing
Typesetting by Sonya Murphy
Printed and bound in China
10 9 8 7 6 5 4

The information presented in this book is intended for general inquiry, research and
informational purposes only and should not be considered as a substitute or replacement
for any trained medical advice, diagnosis, or treatment.

All preparations and information about the usage of botanicals presented in this book are
examples for educational purposes only. Always consult a registered herbalist before taking
or using any preparations suggested in this book for correct identification and safety. No
responsibility will be accepted for the application of the information in this book.

Contents

Welcome, My Tree-loving Friend

book of tree spells! It is rather exciting, and I suppose a little mysterious at the same time, because how does one create a spell with a tree? All my magickal work – actually, all my work – connects the language of plants and their flowers with us. To do this you don't need to collect trees, you just have to collect memories, feelings and an understanding of the way trees live. I am sure you have the wisdom of trees within you already and this will help, but here in my *Book of Tree Spells* I will share with you my research, my findings and my experiences so that you can follow the path of real Nature Magick with me.

Spellwork is energy work, and listening to and understanding the language of plants helps you raise and impart the energy of trees into your spells. If you can sit by a majestic Oak tree, using its fallen leaves to weave your magick, then that would be divine, but if not? I'll show you how to still bring the magick, the love and the power of an Oak tree – of any tree – into your spellcrafting and casting.

To immerse yourself in the world of Tree Magick make sure you are spending mindful time with trees – any tree. Although you may not be able to share time with particular members of each botanical family, all are connected by the universal threads of Nature, so being immersed in their spaces, listening to their language and slowing to the time and pace of trees will ensure you open the door to all.

In your *Book of Tree Spells* I've included sections to help you make and cast spells safely and ethically and I've included instructions on how to create your own spells with trees you already know, those you feel drawn to and those you may need to bring into your life.

I've also shared sixty tree spells that I've crafted just for you from my lifetime collection of research and experiences that are easy to cast and cover a range of everyday situations and challenges. Wishing you a wondrous time exploring the trees and may you find the forest and the trees full of the magick you seek.

Bunches of blessings,
Cheralyn

How to Use This Book

It's never an easy task to create a book of magick instruction to suit everyone. We are all on different paths, with different beliefs and varying levels of experience and I do not believe that these things should bar anyone from experiencing or practising Nature Magick. In order to be safe and work safely for others and your environment, you must first educate yourself in these ways of working. Make sure you read through all the sections of this introduction as it will give you this knowledge. It is simple but vital when creating and casting spells.

Those more experienced in spellcrafting and casting, or who have dedicated and defined paths in their own beliefs, may be able to skim the following instruction pages and dive straight into the spells, experimenting and exploring new paths which may open up, enhance or complement their work. However I suggest that everyone reads through the first section in order to familiarise themselves with the foundations on which I have presented this book of Nature Magick.

Whether you are a complete beginner or have some experience, Section One will provide a good grounding in safe and best practice when creating and casting spells. This section also explains in detail what a spell is and how it works.

I have shared sixty spells that I have written over my life. They focus on trees and their energies and there is a great emphasis on other plants and their flowers. The spells are arranged in smaller chapters by their use so you can quickly find a spell that suits your needs. Make sure you observe the instructions I have given and any instructions you already use each time you are creating and casting spells.

All steps to using each spell are clearly explained along with the simple, everyday ingredients and tools you'll need to create them. I also share interesting and helpful tips with each spell to enrich your experience of working with Nature, so you can get to know our trees a little better.

At the end of this collection, I provide a special journal – a place to keep your own spells. In preparation for creating your own spells, I have included a simple guide to writing your own magick and then a collection of beautiful pages that you may use to keep your tree spells together with mine.

What if you don't have access to your own trees?

As wonderful as it would be to access every tree on earth, no matter where you found yourself, the reality is that you cannot. So I have given you alternatives that you may be able to source and that hold similar energies, but I would also encourage you to dry your own material when available and create or source essences, candles, incenses and other botanical treasures from trusted suppliers so you always have a magickal apothecary to rely on. I've also included a way to create a Magick Proxy Tree in the section 'Ingredients and Tools for Tree Spells', page 11.

What if you don't have trees at all?

I feel it is very important to see the tree to connect with its unique energy. To further focus energy or to connect with trees when you don't have access to them, imagery in the form of artwork, photos, oracle cards or even your own sketches can be used.

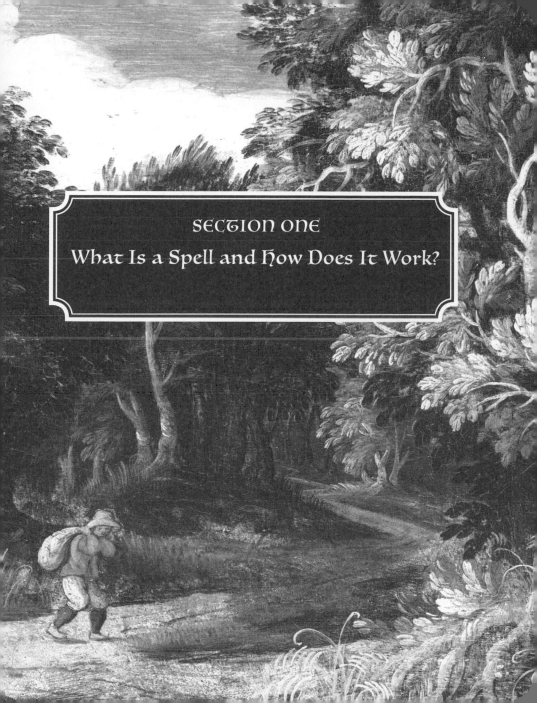

SECTION ONE

What Is a Spell and How Does It Work?

What Is a Spell and How Does It Work?

A spell is a combination of ingredients, tools, actions and focus which come together energetically to create change. Timings (when you cast your spell) can also be observed to ensure added power. These timings can be moon or astrological phases, seasonal times and also correspondences that connect with days of the week or hours of the day or night.

I have included simple, broad timings in this book for moon phase, day of the week and time of day. Observing these will give your spellwork a boost because working in line with the time of Nature is working in synchronicity with what is going on around you and provides stronger focus for your intentions.

The ingredients you gather together to create the spell will all have correspondences to your intention. In a way, they illustrate what it is that you want to happen. They will support the things you wish to happen because they have similar meanings and energies. These meanings and energies may also assist you in removing something. Correspondences also help us find substitute ingredients for our spells when what is written is not available, and I will give you my suggestions with each spell.

For more information about timings and correspondences, see Section 3: How to Create Your Own Tree Spells.

Tools are additional items that you can use to help create your spell. Here are just a few examples of tools used in spellcrafting and casting: cloths to set up your spell on, usually in colours which align with the energy of the spell; wands and staffs to direct and enhance energies; divination tools such as tarot and oracle cards; and crystal balls, pendulums and runes to provide clarity. Bells, music and musical instruments such as drums express your intentions. You may also require practical items such as glasses, cups, vases, bowls and cutting tools.

The way you put a spell together; the words you may recite and the things you actually do to cast your spell are the actions that bring it all together. These focus your intention, put you squarely in front of the path of outcome and strengthen the relationship between the energies of the ingredients and tools you are using. These all combine to raise energy in order for magick to happen.

❧ WHY WOULDN'T A SPELL WORK?

Not many things in life work all the time. External factors influence them; maybe they are not put together properly; sometimes it's just not meant to be. I'm sitting here writing my book for you on my laptop. I love my little computer, but it's rather clunky at times and has had its moments. It closes down for no apparent reason, loses files, can't be bothered accepting my AirDrops and decides I need to look at every file with a certain keyword except the one I want. It appears to have a mind of its own.

You cannot change another person's free will and this is also why spells do not work at times. Perhaps the consequence of the spell will adversely affect another or counter their stronger will, which you might not even be aware of. Another reason a spell may not work is because other energies have greater strength at that moment or they may in fact be leading you to a better eventual outcome.

Spells work because the person creating and casting them fully believes in what they are doing and has a strong, focused intention with a good connection to the energies of their spell and the outcome. While perhaps changing things for personal benefit, the outcome is still generally in keeping with a good outcome for all involved without forcibly changing anyone's free will.

❧ HOW TO CREATE AND CAST A SPELL

When you are using the spells in this book, please ensure you do so safely – and that's not just keeping burning candles well attended. Working with energies to create magick requires you to take responsibility for what you are doing, for yourself and the world you live in. There are many ways you can do

this and there are also ways of life and beliefs which have their own rituals that ensure safety and power in spellcasting.

Most include a way to protect yourself and those around you. A way to mark the beginning of the spell or opening the space is usually next. There will be words, meditation, music, chants or actions which will help you focus on the task at hand and then there will be a way to release the energy, perhaps to give thanks and to close the space. This is a simple and safe way to cast a spell, but you must also read the section Working Magickly with Trees, pages 7–9, to ensure you are working with care and honour.

Timings

I have suggested a moon phase, a day of the week and a time of day to create each spell. These timings are when the energies are in line with the intentions of your spell, so they will give your magickal work additional power. However these suggestions should be seen as a guide only; sometimes a spell is needed immediately and it's best not to wait.

Protect and Open

Before you can begin, it's important to establish protection from negative energies. There are various ways you can achieve this but whatever way you use, make sure you always do it. You may wish to use a smudging method by burning sage or various other plants, or by spraying with a smudging mist. You can also visualise or draw a circle around you and your spell with your finger in the air, then fill your circle with white light. If you are aligned with certain deities, elementals or guides you may wish to ask for their assistance in providing protections as well. A very simple and effective protection method is to light a white candle while visualising the light cleansing, clearing and protecting.

Focus Intention

Sit or stand still for a long moment and imagine your outcome. Really *see* it in your mind and complete your picture with exact times, places and events. At this time, before you cast your spell, you may like to write your intention down and say it out loud to get yourself fully focused and your energy aligned with what you are about to create.

Cast Spell

In each of the tree spells I have shared with you, I have set out very specific steps to create your spell and explained why I've used them. In the final section, I've provided instruction on creating your own spells. 'Casting your spell' is simply what you do to make the spell happen. While casting your spell, you must maintain your focus on your intention.

Release, Close and Ground

Once you have completed your spell, you will need to release the power you have raised in creating it. Releasing the spell will be explained in each spell I share with you, but you can also do this by simply saying: 'I release the power I have raised' or 'It is done' or by putting out your white candle if lit.

'Grounding' is the way you bring yourself back from your spellcasting time. Clapping your hands, ringing a bell or placing your bare feet or hands on the earth are all ways to ground.

❧ WORKING MAGICKLY WITH TREES

» Step one: plant a tree.
» Step two: look after it.

I believe that you can't truly know something unless you do it yourself. And you can't just do it once then forget about it or hire someone to do it for you. In magick this is even more relevant.

There is real magick in doing and in following up and caring for plants. I know as I've seen it for myself and others have written about it for centuries, and I'm sure you have your own experiences as well.

If you do not have a garden, plant the tree somewhere else! Simple. There are no excuses: even in our largest cities there are community gardens, tree-planting days and nature regeneration programs. Go on: off you go and do it now! When you come back I promise you will have the magick right there in your hands.

It's living in the dirt under your nails, it lingers in the scent of leaves in your hair and it lives in the energy you exchanged when you held that plant and put it in the earth. It will grow stronger with each day you check on your tree friend, when you quench its thirst, feed its roots and protect it from harm. When you sit with it and chat, but especially when you are quiet and just listen.

Go and spend time with the family and friends of this tree. Walk through forests; lie under the branches of that tree in the park; stop by the street tree and say hello.

You are now working magickly with trees.

❦ A FEW TREE RESOURCES

To boost your magickal connection, I encourage you to find out a bit more about trees.

Books

Darcey, Cheralyn, *Flowerpaedia: 1000 Flowers and Their Meanings* (Rockpool Publishing, 2017)

Drori, Jonathan, *Around the World in 80 Trees* (Laurence King, 2018)

Hodge, Geoff, *Botany for Gardeners* (Octopus Publishing Group, 2013)

Qing Li, Dr, *Shinrin-Yoku: The Art and Science of Forest-bathing* (Penguin Books Ltd, 2018)

Russell Tony, Cutler Catherine and Walters Martin, *Trees of the World* (Lorenz Books, 2007)

Oracle Deck

Struthers, Jane and Ailwood, Meraylah, *Using the Wisdom of Tree Oracle* (Watkins, 2017)

Websites

Arbor Day Foundation (www.arborday.org)

Kew Gardens (www.kew.org)

Ogham

You may like to explore the Ogham, an ancient alphabet in which names of various trees are associated with individual letters according to the high medieval *Bríatharogam* tradition.

❧ INGREDIENTS AND TOOLS FOR TREE SPELLS

Tools and magickal ingredients can be obtained from bricks-and-mortar stores and online, but always be guided by your feelings when making purchases. Make sure you feel comfortable and positive about these businesses because their energies will transfer.

Anything that comes into your space to use for spellwork has passed through various other hands and should be magickly cleansed. Do this by placing the items under running water, smudging with smoke or placing them underground in suitable wrapping or a container for a night.

Magick harvest

Often, people worry about using flowers, leaves and other organic ingredients in spells because of taking them from living plants for their own needs, and I would say that these botanical treasures are just as precious as the salad you had for lunch. Most of us never give that a second thought, but you should. You should be grateful, mindful and concerned about how the bounty of nature has landed on your plate and you should be giving thanks and giving back to nature in some way as an offering for this kind of physical support.

When obtaining botanical ingredients for magick – or plants and their treasures for any use – you should always follow these steps:

» Never harm the plant.
  Learn how to harvest each type of plant properly.
» Never take more than you need or have a use for.
  Leave some for the next person, animal or time.
» Never harvest more than the plant can sustain sharing.
  You may need to find another plant or source.
» Step lightly in the environment you find yourself in.
  Be mindful of your actions and their possible outcomes.

» Give back to Nature more than you take.

Plant more than you take or help Nature in some way.

» Share what it is you have been blessed with.

You could share your harvest, creation or knowledge.

Create a Magick Proxy Tree

If a spell calls for you to work with a living, growing tree and you do not have access to one, then you may like to create a magick proxy tree instead. All trees, plants and their flowers are connected energetically, and you can call this energy to you. To make it, use a fallen branch of any tree stuck into the earth, with the image of the tree you wish to work with before it, together with any botanicals derived from it (such as oils, essences, leaves and bark) that you have been able to locate. Size will not matter. Once you've created it, say:

Brother, sister, old tree I have faith,

Find the energy of Bodhi,

And bring here to this place.

SECTION TWO
A Collection of Tree Spells

TREE SPELLS FOR
BALANCE AND
HARMONY

Maple Tree Positive Energy Spell

Maples are generally found in temperate northern regions and occasionally subtropical areas of Asia. Mostly deciduous, there are more than 100 species of Maple as well as numerous cultivars.

As well as being a very effective positive energy encourager, Maple leaves can be used in love spells and spells that are crafted to attract abundance and success. The name of this genus, Acer, means 'sharp' and refers to the use of the wood to make spears. It may also refer to the shape of the leaves. This spell will create a handy happiness booster essence that will last for about a week on the shelf or a month in the refrigerator.

Timings
Full Moon, Sunday, Midday

Find and Gather
» a yellow cloth
» a clear glass or crystal bowl – it is preferable to obtain a bowl that you will only use for the making of essences
» 1 cup of rainwater/water
» 4 Maple leaves (*Acer* spp.)
» a glass misting bottle

The Spell

Find a place, ideally outside, where you can leave your essence for a good hour in full sunlight. Lay out your yellow cloth and then place the bowl on it. Slowly pour the water into the bowl and say:

Sparkle water,

Dance in the sun.

Take in the joy,

A new day begun.

Put the Maple leaves into the water one by one, each time saying:

With Maple,

Positive energy be,

With this leaf,

Positive energy free.

Place the essence and leaves in the sunlight for an hour and then strain into the misting bottle. Use each morning in the air of your space (home/work) and repeat the second chant each time. The leaves should be buried in a spot that always has sunshine upon it during the day.

Passing a baby or young child through the branches of a Maple tree will ensure they have a long, happy and healthy life.

Will it rain? If you are lucky enough to be in the vicinity of Maple trees, look at their leaves. If they have turned so that their underside is seen, then a downpour is imminent.

Cedar Tree Gain Control Spell

Although there are many trees bearing the common name 'Cedar', there are only four true Cedars in the world and these are of the Cedrus genus. Perhaps the best-known is the Cedar of Lebanon (Cedrus libani)*, a majestic tree that has been revered since ancient times and is today widely grown as an ornamental tree in parks and gardens.*

The use of cedar in this spell will assist in not only regaining control of situations and yourself by imparting calming energies, clearing and offering protection, but also by providing the strength and wisdom of this large and ancient tree.

Spell boxes can be created for any purpose and are good for issues you feel may be recurring. If you find that at times you lose yourself, emotions or power over situations, then this spell could provide you with a valuable tool.

Timings
Waxing Moon, Tuesday, Midday

Find and Gather
» a black Orchid (*Trichoglottis brachiata*) or any species of Orchid that has a dark colour
» Cedar (*Cedrus* spp.) essential oil

» a small, plain wooden box with a lid – if you can find a Cedarwood box that would be perfect!

» a white fabric bag or cloth to place box in

The Spell

First, let your Orchid dry out completely. This will take about a week.

Place the dried Orchid and the essential oil into your box and say:

In you go, one and then one,

Together combined, for the work to be done.

Close the lid and say:

Magickal box,

Hold and calm,

Bring steady control,

With a thrice times roll.

Rub three drops of the Cedar oil on each side of the box and the lid.

Close and roll it over three times in your hands. Put the box in the white fabric bag/cloth then find a dark, quiet place to keep it. When you would like to experience the magick of your spell to assist in gaining control of a new (or even an old) situation, take the box out and repeat the chant, then roll the box three times.

Used by the Ancient Egyptians for embalming, Cedar oil and wood was prized throughout the ancient world as being incorruptible and therefore sacred. The wood has often been used in the making of boxes for the safekeeping of sacred or valuable texts as well as in the building of religious temples.

The essential oil gained from Cedar is believed to be the very first oil that humans distilled. It is used for its calming, soothing and rejuvenating properties as well as being a very good antiseptic.

Lemon Tree Inspire Joy Spell

Citrus trees originated in south-east Asia from just three types: the mandarin, the pomelo and the citron, so what you find in the citrus world today is the result of years of cultivation and hybridisation. This is thanks to the rare ability citrus trees have to mutate easily as well as the sexual compatibility between the species.

Lemon trees are naturally uplifting and provide a measure of protection as well. This uplifting spell creates a beautiful candle that you could add a gorgeous golden ribbon to and gift to someone needing more joy in their life. Lemon is well known for its cleansing properties so its use will not only impart sparkling joy but clear away dank and dark energies as well.

Timings
Waxing Moon, Friday, Evening

Find and Gather
» a Lemon (*Citrus × limon*)
» a small Lemon tree leaf
» wax/baking paper
» a large yellow or other light-coloured pillar candle

- » a white taper candle
- » a metal spoon

The Spell

Finely grate the zest of the Lemon (just the yellow outer skin) and then air-dry on a plate for a few days before using. Dry the leaf in the same way for a few weeks or by using a flower press. Lay out the wax/baking paper on a heat-proof surface to protect your work area and your candle. Set the pillar candle on the paper. Light the taper candle and drip wax onto the pillar candle. You will need to spread the wax very quickly with the back of the metal spoon. Press the Lemon leaf into the wet wax onto the pillar candle and then melt a little more wax over the top of the leaf and spread with the spoon.

When you have finished, say:

Lemon tree bright,

Clear and make right,

Joy each time,

Your wick is alight.

Once you are happy with the result, melt more taper wax and cover the pillar candle with the dried Lemon zest, finishing with a layer of wax to seal and using the metal spoon to gently spread and push down the pieces into the wax.

To bring joy into an area, to an occasion or a situation, simply light your candle.

While you are drying Lemon zest, you might want to make extra as it is a powerful love charm spell ingredient to help win the affection of the one you desire. The leaves are said to inspire lust when added to teas.

To honour the love of your life and to ensure the longevity of your relationship, grow a Lemon tree from a pip and give it to them.

Bodhi Tree Healing Spell

The Bodhi tree can live up to 2000 years and this attribute may have created its status as a sacred and holy tree in many religions in its native homelands of south-east Asia and India. This is the tree that the Buddha sat beneath when reaching enlightenment.

Bodhi will help you find personal healing. This spell is a walking spell; a way to raise energy to facilitate change. Doing this, as well as focusing energy with a simple meditation on your outcome, will help create a very good all-round healing spell. This could be used to heal rifts in relationships as well as offer support for physical, emotional and mental healing.

Timings

Full Moon, Thursday, Any Time

Find and Gather

» Bodhi tree (*Ficus religiosa*)
» a pink Rose (*Rosa* spp.)
» a spoonful of honey in a beautiful glass

The Spell

Stand in front of the Bodhi tree and say:

> *Brother, sister, old tree I have faith,*
>
> *Find the energy of Bodhi,*
>
> *And bring here to this place.*

Holding the rose, walk around the tree slowly in a clockwise direction. As you walk, gently loosen the petals and let them drift to the earth. As each petal falls to the ground, say:

> *The circle of healing grows in the dirt,*
>
> *Healing will come from deep in the earth.*

Repeat until all petals have been released and your circle is formed, then take the honey and pour it onto the bark of the tree, and say:

> *A gift of thanks, for work to be done.*

Sit down, close your eyes and focus on the way you would like to see the situation, person, animal or thing healed. Stay as long as you feel you need to. Leave the petals to do as nature pleases with them.

Walking around a Bodhi tree can also rid you of evil influences. You will need to do this at least three times but it should drive away any negative entities that are attracted to you.

A folklore cure for female infertility in many Asian countries involves walking naked around a Bodhi tree.

Blackthorn Tree Remove Negativity Spell

A very common wild shrub throughout Europe, the Blackthorn produces fruit that are used to make jams, syrups and wines. Another name for both the tree and its fruit is 'Sloe'. The fruit is also traditionally used to produce the drink sloe gin.

Not only will Blackthorn help remove negative energies, it will also stabilise emotions and reveal hope for you going forward. This spell creates a somewhat bitter though refreshing drink to clear away negative energies. When you drink your magickal sparkling brew make sure that you visualise the negativity you are trying to get rid of, leaving.

Timings
Waning Moon, Saturday, Midnight/Dusk

Find and Gather

» 3 Blackthorn sloes (*Prunus spinose*) – if unobtainable replace with any dark edible fruit but also use an image of Blackthorn
» 2 tablespoons of lemon juice
» a wooden spoon
» a beautiful clear glass
» 1 teaspoon of honey
» champagne or sparkling wine or water

The Spell

Prick the sloes and soak them in the lemon juice overnight. The next day, squash the sloes into the juice with the spoon and then strain, retaining the juice. Say:

Juice of Blackthorn,

Bitter and sour,

The things that have darkened me,

Will go with this hour.

Bury the fruit in a dark place in the garden.

Pour the juice into the glass and say:

Magickal juice,

With each sip this will end.

Negative leaves,

While positive mends.

Add the honey and stirring say:

Sweet mender and healer mix well.

Top with the champagne or sparkling or wine or water and say:

Bubble and fizz,

Alive is the brew.

The Dark disappear,

The Light is anew!

Drink all but a mouthful and throw this out the front door, saying:

And now be forever gone!

The wood of the Blackthorn is traditionally used in Ireland in the making of shillelaghs. These sticks are used as both walking sticks and magickal wands.

Thorn trees have strong links with faeries and Blackthorn have their own guardians, the Luantishees. These faeries have their own special day, 11 November, and on this day black ribbons tied around the trunks of Blackthorns and blessings of gratitude for their work are greatly appreciated. However, you must never harvest anything from a Blackthorn tree on this day, as to do so will cause great harm to come to you.

Holly Tree Find Balance Spell

The evergreen Holly is native to Europe as well as western Asia. It is a smaller understory tree that thrives in shaded woodland. Synonymous with Christmas, it also was — and still is — an important Pagan tree that is a symbol of life and renewal as part of midwinter observances. Holly shares the energies of peace, protection and cheerfulness and can help with finding balance.

Witch Bottles, also known as Spell Bottles, have been in use since at least the early 17th century in the UK and USA. They can be created for any purpose, but I particularly like making Witch Bottles that symbolise your challenges and provide a focus point for you to watch. Whatever you place inside, how it reacts when shaken will be like all the pieces mixing up and then settling in your own personal puzzle.

Timings
Full Moon, Wednesday, Twilight

Find and Gather
- 12 Holly leaves (*Ilex aquifolium*)
- a beautiful clear bottle and cap
- 6 red beads

- » 2 tablespoons of rosewater
- » a stone from the garden
- » water

The Spell

Divide the Holly leaves into two piles of six leaves each before you and say:

Balanced before me and balanced shall be.

Add them to the bottle and say:

Twelve leaves of the Holly,

Dance, play and just be,

But always dear Holly,

Find balance for me.

Add the red beads, the rosewater and water to fill and say:

Guiding love and true heart.

Add the stone and say:

Grounded balance will start.

Seal the bottle. Whenever you are seeking balance, simply shake the bottle then sit quietly and watch the contents completely settle. You should receive thoughts that will help you ground and be more balanced. This bottle will last about a month before the contents degrade. Empty and clean well then create a new Witch Bottle.

The origin of the festive wreath on the front door at Christmas time is in the practice of hanging Holly wreaths on doors to provide a place for Faeries and wood spirits in midwinter. This would also ensure good luck for the coming year.

To bless your garden, try holding nine holly berries out under the light of a Full Moon for an hour. Pop them into a glass of beer (*DO NOT DRINK! Holly berries are poisonous!*) and then pour it over your garden. This potion is said to improve the qualities of the blossoms of any plant but particularly those of Foxgloves and Hollyhocks.

Linden Tree Remove Stress Spell

The most outstanding feature of this widespread Northern Hemisphere native is its huge heart-shaped leaves. These, combined with its gorgeous, highly perfumed flowers, make Linden a popular street and parkland tree in that part of the world. The inner bark (liber) was once used as a form of paper and is where the word 'library' comes from.

Linden provides soothing energies for this spell. The creation of your own teas is something magickal all by itself. Finding botanicals that you are drawn to and mixing them together to make warming drinks to delight, calm and please you is real kitchen magick. Here you will be adding a few chants to empower a selection of botanicals that I have found personally beneficial for stress removal. If you cannot find Linden flowers, you may like to try Chamomile.

Timings
Waning Moon, Saturday, Midnight/Dusk

Find and Gather

» 1 cup dried Linden flowers (*Tilia* spp.)
» ½ cup Lemon Balm leaves (*Melissa officinalis*)
» 2 dried heads of Lavender flowers (*Lavandula* spp.)
» an airtight container
» boiling water

» a beautiful teapot and cups

» honey

» a few Linden tree twigs (*if possible*)

The Spell

Place the Linden flowers, Lemon Balm leaves and Lavender flower heads (intact) in the airtight container and leave for about a week so that the fragrances and tastes can combine.

As you pop them in, say:

Linden and Lavender

So healing and calming,

Together with Balm,

So lovely and soothing.

When you wish to use, add 2 tablespoons for each cup of the mixed Linden flowers and Lemon Balm leaves to your teapot. (Leave the Lavender in the container as an aromatic flavouring to your tea.) Add enough boiling water for each cup. Leave to stand for a few minutes. Turn the pot clockwise three times and say:

Calm come in,

Stress go out.

Pour, sweeten with honey if desired, stir with a Linden twig, then sip slowly.

Planting a Linden tree in your home's garden will offer protection for everyone within. The branches can be cut (*or fallen ones used*) and placed over the front and back doors to prevent evil and misfortune entering.

The bark and branches of Linden trees are considered very lucky and Linden leaves, also edible, are used in spells for immortality. You might like to add a leaf or two to your tea mixture.

Rowan Tree Energy Protection Spell

The Rowan tree is a native of Europe and Asia and is often found near sacred sites, especially stone circles throughout the UK and Ireland. Legend tells us that it grows 'thrice as well' in these places. Common names for this tree include Witch Tree, Wicken and Witchbeam, all indications of its long history as an important tree of magick. Rowan is regarded as an all-round protection tree.

An amulet is a magickal object that contains energies, usually to protect the holder, so they should be carried. This spell requires you to create such an amulet from items that will offer energy protection. I find this very helpful if I am going to places where I am sharing what I do, or going to places that are very busy or contain too much negative or drawing energy.

Timings
Full Moon, Saturday, Late Night

Find and Gather
» a Rowan tree or the photo of a Rowan tree (*Sorbus aucuparia*)
» pencil and paper
» a small gold bag

- » 3 Rowan leaves
- » 3 White Sage leaves (*Salvia apiana*)
- » 3 Basil leaves (*Ocimum basilicum*)

The Spell

Traditionally this type of amulet would have contained three Rue leaves (*Ruta graveolens*). As Rue can cause severe dermatitis on contact with skin and the charm bag will be worn or carried, I replace Rue with White Sage.

If you have access to a Rowan tree, sit before it and draw it using the pencil and paper. If not, find a suitable photo of a Rowan tree to draw, and say:

Alive on the paper,
Witch Tree you will be,
Protect my energy,
For all and for me.

Fold the artwork three times and place in the gold bag. Add the leaves. Carry it with you to provide protection of your energy in times of need. To use, close your eyes and touch the amulet bag. Visualise your energy as a huge bubble around you, transparent but strong and unbroken — any corruption or hole you have felt in it, repaired. Place the bag next to your ear for a few moments. If you ever feel you need to replace this amulet for any reason, bury it in a cool dark place away from your home or workplace.

If you would like to ensure a successful flower garden, collect Rowan berries on Rowan Tree Day (*1 May*) and fill an old leather boot or shoe with them. Bury in your flower bed on Wednesday or Friday.

Carrying the berries or the wood of Rowan is said to heighten psychic abilities and intuition, while a staff or walking stick of Rowan will not only offer protection but ensure you do not become lost.

English Oak Tree Inner Strength Spell

Living for hundreds of years, the mighty English, or European, Oak tree is a haven for many woodland birds and animals. All Oak tree species have been celebrated as symbols of grounding, longevity and strength throughout time by many faiths.

In this spell you will be tapping into the strength of the Oak tree. Using a candle of a colour that corresponds with strength will further empower your spell. This spell could easily be cast using items from any large, powerful tree in your area, but check the meanings and attributes of the tree first.

Timings
Full Moon, Sunday, Midday

Find and Gather
» a large flat tray
» a cup of sand (*Note: if it's
   illegal to take sand from the
   beach in your area, sand
   can be purchased from
   home-improvement and art
   and craft stores*)
» an Oak twig (*Quercus
   robur*)

- » a red candle
- » a candle holder
- » matches
- » an acorn

The Spell

Set your tray before you, pour the sand onto it and say:

> Sand from the earth,
>
> Sand from the sea,
>
> Ground and protect,
>
> What is within me.

With the Oak twig, draw the outline of an Oak leaf and say:

> Strong and steadfast,
>
> Leaf of the tree,
>
> Within you lives a strength,
>
> That will grow within me.

Place the red candle in its holder in the centre of the Oak leaf outline and light. Hold the acorn in front of the flame and say three times:

> Light from the Oak,
>
> Light from the flame.

Let the candle burn completely out. Carry the acorn with you when you need a boost in inner strength. All ingredients used in this spell (except for the tray and candle holder) should be buried under a large tree when complete.

The shape of modern blind-pulls is not accidental. It is believed Oak trees protect against lightning strikes. Blind-pulls may be shaped like acorns and other decorative window elements were often made of Oak or embellished with Oak motifs for this reason.

Hollow Oak trees are thought to be the home of Faeries, Elves and woodland spirits. In Ireland and Scotland these trees are known as 'Bell Oaks' and in England as 'Bull Oaks'.

Elm Tree Psychic Attack Shield Protection

Elm, being one of the few woods that do not rot in water, has been used to make ships, bearing posts in buildings and pipes. This tree dominated the European landscape until the Dutch Elm disease (first recorded in 1910) severely reduced the population of most species over time.

Elm has very strong grounding energies and also offers stability. The use of loud noises in spells will often indicate the beginning or end of the spell, however in this spell sound is used as a correspondence. Imitating thunder, the sound of lightning, is meant to frighten off the negative energy you may have experienced or are trying to avoid. It is believed in many folklores that Elm trees are never struck by lightning as they have command and power over it.

Timings

New Moon, Sunday, Midnight

Find and Gather

- » a large shallow bowl
- » rainwater
- » pen and paper
- » a large metal saucepan
- » a large metal spoon
- » a good handful of Elm leaves (*Ulmus* spp.)

Elm, Hyde Park, London.

The Spell

Fill the bowl with water and say:

Water of storms,

Of sky and clouds.

Swirl the water around briskly.

Use the pen and paper to write down your psychic attack experience or simply write that you wish to be protected from a psychic attack. This spell will last a month.

Rip up the paper and drop it into the water while swirling it briskly again, and say:

Take this attack,

Reversed it shall be.

Bang the saucepan with the spoon three times. This represents the sound of thunder. Throw the Elm leaves into the air so they fall around you and say:

Surround me with protection,

Create your great shield.

Elm tree I ask you,

To look after me.

Pour the water onto the ground and dig the paper into the earth. Bang the saucepan with the spoon three more times.

Elves are said to be fond of the Elm tree and this has led to the common name of Elven for Elms in some areas. The reputation of the tree and its wood for never being struck by lightning is perhaps because Elves offer this protection.

References to Elm can be found in the stories of the Roman god of wine, Bacchus. The planting and pollarding of this tree in vineyards throughout time in many areas is due to the belief that these are the best trees to offer shade, support and protection to the growing vines.

TREE SPELLS
FOR MODERN
PROBLEMS

Larch Tree Social Media Protection Spell

The European Larch tree is a long-lived conifer that thrives at high altitudes. A native of Europe, it is found from the Southern Alps through to the Carpathian Mountains. It is also a popular forestry tree throughout North America and Europe.

Larch is a brilliant self-confidence booster and helps dissolve negativity. Creating the symbol of a cross in spells can mean that you are crossing the path or blocking the way of something. In this spell you make this symbol to stop or slow the effects of negative social media activity. Another wood can be substituted but you must use Larch or at least Pine (Pinus spp.) needles for this spell to work.

Timings
Waning Moon, Saturday, Midnight/Dusk

Find and Gather
» Larch wood (*Larix decidua*) – 2 small twigs or pieces of wood, any size you desire
» black string – length to suit
» 3 Larch needles (*leaves*)

THE EUROPEAN LARCH.

The Spell

Take the two pieces of Larch wood and hold them in front of your computer screen in the form of a cross. Bind in the middle with the black string and say:

Social media,

Stay good and stay true,

This cross to stop,

Harm and undue influence.

Place the three Larch needles in the centre of your cross, bind them with the black string and say:

Leaves that are sharp,

Leaves that are three,

Together watch over,

And repel negativity.

Place in front of your computer screen and leave. If you think it needs a boost at any time, burn dried Larch and pass through the smoke. Use this on phones and tablets by tapping the screen with the cross three times each morning.

Due to the belief that Larch wood was impervious to fire, it was and still is used to create amulets and talisman that offer protection from fire and enchantment, and to ward off the 'evil eye'.

In Siberian mythology, the first man is said to have been created from a Larch tree. To the Lapp and Siberian people, Larch is considered to be the 'World-tree'. This is a tree in many religions and beliefs that is thought to hold up and support the heavens and be a connection of sorts between heaven and earth – and sometimes the otherworld below.

Alder Tree Dispute Shield Spell

The Alder tree grows best close to waterways throughout Europe, where it enjoys damp, even waterlogged, marshy grounds. The timber produced from Common Alder (Black Alder) is water-resistant and was used for the foundations of many buildings in the water-filled city of Venice in Italy. Other uses included boat-building and bridge piles.

Alder provides shielding and helps release negative and destructive energies. This spell creates a water mist to be sprayed around you to provide shielding from disagreements. It would be very beneficial in the workplace or in social circles when you do not wish to become involved with the disputes of others.

Alnus.

Timings

Waning Moon, Tuesday, Midday

Find and Gather

» 1 cup of pure water
» a large crystal/glass bowl
» Alder (*Alnus glutinosa*) – a twig, leaf, seed or other Alder-based botanical
» a glass misting bottle

The Spell

Find a place, preferably outside, where you can leave your essence for an hour in the sunlight.

Pour the pure water into the bowl and say:

Water of emotion,

You will hold and shield.

Place your Alder wood or other Alder items in the water and say:

As Alder resists,

So might I.

Troubles meant for others,

Will not find me.

Leave in the sunlight for an hour, then strain the essence water into your misting bottle. Use each morning in the air of your space (home/work) when you know disputes are imminent or when they occur. Repeat the last four lines of the chant each time.

If you wish to use the Alder pieces for another purpose, first dry them in the sunlight and smudge them to cleanse.

The term 'Alderman' comes to us from the common name of this tree. It is derived from 'ealdor', the old English word for chief. The red dye obtained from the tree was also used as a ritual face paint for sacred kings in ancient times.

Three different dyes are obtained from the Common Alder tree: red from the bark, brown from the twigs and green from the leaves and flowers.

Hazel Tree Study Spell

Hazel can be classified as either a tree or a shrub, but most experts agree that it is a tree as it can reach the 6-metre (20-foot) height requirement. However, it has low branches like a shrub. Found growing naturally across Europe, western Asia and North Africa, this is the tree that produces the widely consumed Hazelnut.

Hazel is a tree of knowledge and skill with words. In this spell you will be combining the learning- and focus-enhancing qualities of the crystal green fluorite with the energies of the Hazel tree — leaving you with a little study snack as well!

Timings
Waxing, Wednesday, Daytime

Find and Gather
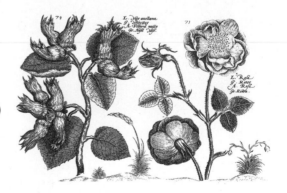

» a baking tray
» baking paper
» 1 cup of raw hulled Hazelnuts (*Corylus avellana*)
» clean tea towel
» a violet candle
» a candle holder
» matches
» a green fluorite crystal bracelet

The Spell

First you will need to roast the Hazelnuts.

Preheat oven to 180°C (385°F). Line the baking tray with baking paper and spread out the whole Hazelnuts in a single layer. Roast for 10 minutes or until lightly toasted and the skins have started to crack.

Remove the skins. To do this, place Hazelnuts in a clean tea towel and gently rub together until the skins come away. As you rub, say:

Wisdom and knowledge,

Warm within me.

Set up your study area by lighting the violet candle in its holder and placing the green fluorite crystal bracelet in front of it. Take one Hazelnut and crush it.

Sprinkle a tiny bit carefully into the flame and say:

Alive the words, ideas and concepts,

I promise to do my very best.

Put the bracelet on and commence your study. Let the candle burn down. You can nibble the rest of the Hazelnuts for a study mind-power boost as you work. Wear the bracelet at any other time to ensure good study sessions, and in exams and during assessments so that the knowledge you gained while studying is in focus again.

Hazel trees are said to be portals and doorways into the Faerie world. It is said that Wild Thyme, olive oil, Rose and Marigold water mixed with the buds of young Hazel can be used to open the way.

May Day is the traditional day to gather Hazel wood that can be used to create protective talismans. The use of Hazel wood to create hurdles around farms in many parts of the world probably stems from this belief as well.

Baobab Tree Traveller Spell

An African native tree, the Baobab is one of the widest trees in the world. The hollow trunk becomes swollen with water, attaining a circumference of up to 30 metres (100 feet) while holding up to 1200 litres (2540 pints) of water.

You will be crafting a tiny Baobab tree trunk using a Walnut shell as a base. This talisman can be easily slipped into a cotton crotchet crystal holder. You can also place the talisman in your bag or suitcase. Walnut shells make excellent natural lockets as they are guardians of magick. The crystal malachite is used in this spell for its ability to offer protection to travellers, ward off the evil eye and for the additional gift of helping those who fear flying.

Timings
Full Moon, Thursday, Midday

Find and Gather
» a Baobab tree (*Adansonia digitata*) – or an image and (*if possible*) any part from a Baobab tree (*essence, leaves, bark, twigs*)
» water

- » two clean dry Walnut shell halves (*Juglans regia*)
- » a very small malachite crystal
- » strong glue
- » crotchet crystal holder or tiny mojo bag – optional

The Spell

Either sit beneath a Baobab tree or create a little shrine to the tree with an image and the Baobab tree parts.

Pour the water into one Walnut shell half and say:

Travel well within this shell.

Where we go, travel well.

Pour this water into the other Walnut shell half and say:

To return safe, so it will be.

Pour the water on the ground and say:

Come back to here, safe.

Place the Walnut shells somewhere they can air-dry for a day and place the malachite crystal in one half. When completely dry, glue the two shells together, retaining the crystal inside, and leave to dry as per the glue instructions. You may like to decorate or paint the closed shells or cover them in air-dry clay. Wear when travelling or place in your luggage.

The kings and elders of Africa would hold their meetings under Baobab trees as they felt that the tree's spirit would guide them in their work and decisions. To this day, this tree is used as a community meeting place in many regions.

Known also as 'upside-down' trees due to their appearance, Baobabs are in fact the largest succulent plant in the world. Because they hollow out to store water, their trunks have been used as shelter and some have been used as shops or bars.

Coconut Palm Tree Relaxation Spell

Extensively naturalised in warmer climes throughout the world, the Coconut Palm was originally native to the Eastern Tropics. They can grow to 18 metres (60 feet) and are planted not only for their beautiful appearance but for their usefulness, as every part of this remarkable tree can be utilised. The fruit as a food, drink and an oil of many uses; the leaves and trunk for construction; the flower as a base for a type of wine called 'toddy'; and the Coconut fruit husks as a fuel and textile matting.

This spell creates a gorgeous oil that can be used directly on the skin or added to a bath.

Use this oil when you are feeling stressed, nervous or apprehensive. The addition of Rose will give you some additional love and peace.

Timings
Waning Moon, Monday, Midnight

Find and Gather
» a Palm leaf (*any type*) – if you cannot obtain one, be crafty: for example, create one from paper
» a clear glass/crystal bowl
» a rose quartz crystal
» 1 cup Coconut oil (*Cocos nucifera*) – carefully melted in a double boiler

» 11 drops of Rose essential oil (*Rosa* spp.)

» a beautiful bottle, sterilised

The Spell

In a quiet place, put your Palm leaf on the ground and the bowl upon it. Place the rose quartz crystal in the bowl and then gently pour the Coconut oil into the bowl while breathing softly and deeply over the bowl to bring calming energy into the space.

Drop the Rose oil into the bowl, stir in an anti-clockwise direction, and say:

Relax, relax, relax.

Take three deep breaths and then stir clockwise, and say:

Relax, relax, relax.

Take out the crystal then pour the oil mixture into the bottle and store in a cool dry place out of direct sunlight.

The people of Samoa share the myth that the Coconut Palm originally grew at the entrance to the spirit world and was known as 'Leosia', 'the spirit watcher'. If a spirit struck the tree, they would return to the mortal world.

You can provide protection to your home or any building by hanging a fresh coconut in a high place within. Another method is to drain the coconut of its milk and then fill with herbs that provide protective qualities. Seal and bury next to the place where you require protective energies.

Jacaranda Tree Lucky Money Spell

This fast-growing tree is a favourite street tree in suitable climates. Jacaranda is native to Paraguay, southern Brazil and northern Argentina. The mauve-blue flowers completely cover the tree before falling to create a colourful carpet below.

Jacaranda brings with it the meanings and energies of wisdom, luck and also a bit of love! In this spell, you will also be using Basil as it is a naturally lucky herb and also a good friend of money. The use of a citrine crystal will help with prosperity.

Timings
Full Moon, Thursday, Morning

Find and Gather
- » a green candle
- » a candle holder
- » 3 gold coins
- » 3 citrine crystals
- » a beautiful box with a lid

» a handful of dried Basil (*Ocimum basilicum*)

» Jacaranda flowers (*Jacaranda mimosifolia*)

The Spell

Place the green candle in the holder in front of the box and light. Pop the coins into the box, add the citrine crystals and say:

> *Golden coins and crystals gold,*
>
> *Glow with growth within.*

Sprinkle in the Basil and say:

> *Abundance and success,*
>
> *Grow for me and do your best.*

Sprinkle in the Jacaranda flowers and say:

> *Wisdom and luck,*
>
> *So it will be.*

When you wish to boost your luck with money, open the box and ask for it. Keep your box in a private, quiet and dark place to protect the energies.

The Amazonia Moon Goddess visited earth as a beautiful bird named Mitu who landed upon a Jacaranda tree. She spent her time living with the people and sharing wisdom and knowledge with them. When her time was over, she ascended through the Jacaranda, covered in flowers.

In many parts of the world, if a Jacaranda bloom falls on your head it is considered to be good luck. A modern Australian superstition suggests that if you have not begun your study for final exams by the time the Jacarandas bloom, it is too late.

White Mulberry Tree Wholeness Spell

Native to northern China, this tree is the food source of silkworms. While the fruit of the White Mulberry is edible, it is the Black Mulberry (Morus nigra) that produces the berries most people are familiar with.

This is a spell for those who feel they might not be as healthy as they would like to be. White Mulberry will provide harmony and help with connecting with what it is you may need for yourself to achieve wholeness. The colour turquoise is used in this spell as it is associated with wholeness, emotional balance, spiritual grounding and patience.

Timings
Full Moon, Monday, Morning

Find and Gather

» A few White Mulberry leaves (*Morus alba*)
» a tree
» a real silk scarf, hanky, tie or ribbon – preferably turquoise or white
» a ball of white string
» a pair of scissors
» a fire

The Spell

If you do not have the leaves, create some from paper and have an image of the White Mulberry tree nearby. Go to your tree and tie your silk item to it. Tie one end of your ball of string to the tree also. Walk away from the tree while unwinding the ball of string, saying:

Away I go and all I will see,
From small to larger,
What I need released to be me.

Walk as far as you can without losing sight of the tree, taking the leaves with you.

When you are happy, drop the leaves on the ground and then walk back and wind the string that has been released from the ball back into your hand, making a new ball. Cut the string so you have two string balls.

Create your fire, making sure it is safe. (Perhaps in a cauldron or a fire-proof bowl.)

Throw the new ball of string on the fire and say out loud all the things you want to release so you can be whole. Take the rest of the string and wind it around the tree three times. Cut the end. Place this string under your pillow with your silk item. You should dream of ways to healthy wholeness.

Wear your silk item when you are seeking healthy outcomes, paths and answers.

In 1608, King James I of England was keen to establish a silk industry so encouraged the planting of Mulberry trees throughout England. The story goes that people did just that but unfortunately for the industry, planted Black Mulberry (*M. nigra*) which produces the more delicious fruit but is not the tree that supports silkworms.

Mulberry is a very good protector against evil in any form and also makes a powerful wand that can be used in general spellcasting as well as protection, exorcism and magickal cleansing work.

Eucalyptus Tree Stop Me Texting Spell

*All native to the Southern Hemisphere, with most being also evergreen,
there are over 400 species of Eucalyptus. The timber is widely used and
the tree grown also for its beauty and fast-growing habit in temperate
locations throughout the world.*

*A modern dilemma is how to stop yourself texting, messaging or posting
updates on social media at times when you probably shouldn't. In this
spell, the use of Eucalyptus helps to bring in the energies of division
between worlds, ideas and places and is a purifier. You are also smudging
by using the smoke of the eucalyptus and protecting with the energies of
this tree through its image.*

Timings
Waning, Wednesday, Midnight

Find and Gather

- » a heat-proof dish
- » pen and paper
- » matches
- » dried Eucalyptus leaves
  (*Eucalyptus* spp.)
- » a digital image of a
  Eucalyptus tree
- » your phone

The Spell

Set up your heat-proof dish outside.

On the piece of paper, write down the last few texts, messages or social media posts that you sent but wish you hadn't. Drop into the dish, set them carefully alight and say:

The last of my words,

I cannot undo,

This day forward,

I wish to be true.

Empty the ashes out onto the ground and stamp them in with your feet.

Place the Eucalyptus leaves in the dish and set them alight.

Pass your phone very carefully through the smoke and say:

Cleanse out the things,

I've done before.

Stop me from doing this any more.

Keep the image of the Eucalyptus tree on your phone and in times of need, set it as your screensaver. It will help stop you from texting, messaging and posting when you probably shouldn't.

Eucalyptus trees are natural purifiers and will assist with rejuvenation, healing, gaining clarity, and mental focus. They can also help to boost your immune and energy systems. Perhaps one of the easiest ways is via Eucalyptus oil, which can be used in aromatherapy preparations and in various direct applications.

The leaves of Eucalyptus change shape over the tree's lifetime. While young, the leaves stand out horizontality to collect maximum light. As the tree ages, the leaves twist so that they present vertical to the tree, protecting it from too much heat radiation and light.

Coral Tree Job Hunting Spell

An incredibly fast-growing tree that is a native to Brazil, most of the Coral Tree is covered in thick thorns. It produces beautiful downward-hanging flower panicles. Each of these appear in six-week cycles and can contain up to 100 flowers.

The use of Coral Tree in a job hunting spell is due to the energies of positivity and confidence and its ability to help you to stay focused on what it is you are trying to achieve. If you cannot find Coral Tree flowers, substitute Coral Tree essence sprinkled over red Rose petals. I have given timings which will provide you with a really important booster but you can and should do this spell on the first day of each week while you are job hunting. The especially keen may like to do it every job-hunting day.

Timings
New Moon, Wednesday, Sunrise

Find and Gather

» a handful of Coral Tree flowers (*Erythrina* spp.), fresh or dried
» a big handful of multi-coloured flower petals and leaves, fresh or dried
» a beautiful bowl
» a compass

The Spell

The night before the spell, place the Coral Tree flowers and the multi-coloured flower petals and leaves in the bowl and say:

A celebration awaits,

When I return to my gates.

Place the compass on top of the botanicals and say:

Take me to where my new job awaits.

In the morning, before you leave for the day, walk out your front door with the bowl for a few paces, turn around and start to walk back while throwing the botanicals into the air and saying three times:

The next time I return,

A job I will have earned.

Take one Coral Tree petal and place it in your pocket or bag to take with you for additional luck.

Thought to be *E. variegate*, a Coral Tree is found in Tibetan Buddhism as the tree referred to as 'man da ra ba' in Sukhavati. In the Hindu faith, it is believed that the Mandarah tree in Indra's garden in Svarga is a Coral Tree (*E. stricta*).

Many Coral Trees are used as supporting plants for crops. Some are used to provide shade for Coffee and Cocoa plantations while others provide support for climbing vines such as the Vanilla Orchid.

Walnut Entrepreneur Spell

The Walnut tree has been widely cultivated for both its beautiful timber and delicious nuts. The Romans introduced the Walnut to Britain and from there it was taken to the USA and beyond. Its natural distribution spreads from Greece through to central China and Japan.

This spell will create a type of Florida Water with the added energy of Walnut. This tree will help support you as you head for change or forge new relationships. It will give you inner strength and provide fertile ground and longevity. In many communities, especially those connected with the practice of Vodoun, Florida Water is a powerful spiritual protector and cleanser. Not for consumption, it can be used lightly as a personal fragrance, added to a bath or sprinkled around your place of business or work.

Timings

Waxing Moon, Thursday, Daytime

Find and Gather

- » 1 Walnut (*Juglans regia*), crushed – or about a teaspoon
- » 2 cups of vodka
- » 2 tablespoons of Orange Flower water (*Citrus sinensis*)

- » 2 drops of Jasmine essential oil (*Jasminum officinale*)
- » 16 drops of Bergamot essential oil (*Citrus bergamia*)
- » 12 drops of Lavender essential oil (*Lavandula* spp.)
- » 3 drops of Lemon essential oil (*Citrus × limon*)
- » 2 drops of Rose attar essential oil (*Rosa* spp.)
- » a gorgeous bottle, sterilised

The Spell

Mix all ingredients together and place in the bottle while saying:

Ventures I'm taking,
Plans I will make,
Success will come to me,
Each day as I wake.

Use as needed to provide protection and to ensure success to your business endeavours.

You may find it useful to use at the beginning of your working week and again at times when you are attending important meetings, making decisions or working on anything especially challenging.

If you wish to use on your skin as a fragrance, do a small patch test on your inner arm first and monitor for 24 hours. Adding to a sterilised spray bottle can also make it easier to use.

Traditionally, ink has been made from Walnuts and it makes a very magickal way to write your own spells or keep your journal or Book of Shadows. You can also use it to stain wood.

The Walnut is often referred to as the 'Tree of Prophecy' or 'The Royal Tree', as the health of the tree would foretell the fortune of those residing nearby. For example if the tree fell, it was a very bad sign.

TREE SPELLS FOR
RELATIONSHIPS
AND LOVE

Myrrh Tree Divorce Ritual

From eastern and north-eastern tropical Africa, the bark of the Myrrh tree produces a resin prized as an incense, in perfumes, as a flavouring in food and as a complementary healing ingredient. More of a shrub than a tree, it is covered in thorns and will only grow in full sun.

Myrrh will bring the energies of emotional balance, healing and wisdom so will help with any stage of a divorce in which you need support. Cyclamen flowers assist us to say goodbye and to leave a situation cleanly. Cyclamen plants are poisonous so please take care when using in this spell. Beware of the place you are planting the cyclamen and keep out of the reach of young children and pets.

Timings
Waning Moon, Saturday, Midnight

Find and Gather
» a Cyclamen plant (*Cyclamen* spp.)
» a plant pot and potting mix
» a heat-proof dish
» matches
» a charcoal disc or block
» Myrrh resin (*Commiphora myrrha*)
  – a few small pieces

The Spell

This spell needs to be done in a place where you and the person you wish to separate peacefully from have both been together. Carefully replant the Cyclamen in the new pot and say:

It is time for goodbye,

I wish us to part,

But peacefully go,

And make a new start.

Place the charcoal disc on the heat-proof dish and light it. Place the myrrh on the glowing charcoal. Pass the dish over and around the cyclamen plant and say:

Separate calm,

Peaceful we go.

Leave the Cyclamen in the place you planted it for seven nights and then gift it to the person you are parting with. If you cannot do that, place it at the back door, in the rear yard or towards the back of your home.

The ancient Egyptian ruler Queen Hatshepsut was one of the first plant hunters and would send out expeditions to Somalia to collect the resin of the Myrrh tree to be burned in the temples.

Myrrh used as an incense provides a very conducive atmosphere for deeper meditations. It can also be used to help heal grief and sorrow and to connect with the dead.

Flowering Dogwood Tree Boundary Spell

Common in its native North America and Europe, the Flowering Dogwood is noted for its bark. The trunk will fissure as the tree grows, splitting into small, square blocks. What appear to be white flowers are actually large, long bracts surrounding much smaller clusters of green flowers.

Dogwood provides purity and helps set boundaries. Mirrors are a good means of creating a boundary of protection by bouncing back and deflecting any negative energies. Used together, you can cast a spell to quickly disperse unwanted intrusions into your world.

Timings
Waning Moon, Saturday, Midday

Find and Gather
» a black cloth
» a mirror
» 4 black candles
» candle holders – if required
» matches
» pencil and paper
» 4 flowers or leaves of the Flowering Dogwood (*Cornus florida*)

The Spell

Lay out the black cloth and place the mirror in the centre.

Place the candles around the mirror, forming a square, and say:

> *All that falls on the silver light,*
> *Protected within the boundary right.*

On the paper, write down what it is that you are seeking boundary protection for. Fold the paper and place it in the centre of the mirror.

Place the Dogwood flowers or leaves next to each candle and say:

> *Tree of Dogwood,*
> *Pure and bright,*
> *Hold what is within,*
> *All safe and tight.*

Dry out the flowers or leaves and bury near the entrance to your property.

The boundaries of Rome were created by Romulus using his javelin which he then threw at Palatine Hill. It landed and took root, becoming a Dogwood tree. It was also a popular timber for the creation of weapons such as spears during Ancient Roman times.

Collecting a little sap from a Dogwood tree during midsummer in a handkerchief creates a talisman that will help your wishes come true. Carry it with you always to ensure this.

Italian Cypress Tree Peaceful Separation Spell

The Italian Cypress has a distinctive tall column-like appearance. These are the trees that are synonymous with Tuscany as they grace the rolling hills of this Italian landscape. Unlike other Cedars, the leaves of the Italian Cypress have no scent.

The Cypress tree helps us find our personal path and can help lead us out of difficult or unwanted situations. It can also help support you through the mourning of loss and departure. This spell creates a relaxing bath salt blend that can help release and soften negative feelings surrounding a separation. The addition of Rose petals will further support you with courage and love. This spell makes about just over a cup of magickal bath salts.

Timings
Full Moon, Monday, Evening

Find and Gather
» 1 cup of Himalayan salts
» ¼ cup of bicarbonate of soda
» a glass mixing bowl
» 1 teaspoon of dried Rose petals (*Rosa* spp.)
» 5 drops of Lavender essential oil (*Lavandula* spp.)

» 11 drops of Cypress essential oil (*Cupressus* spp.)

» a wooden spoon

» a gorgeous jar

» an image of the Tuscan landscape featuring Italian Cypress trees (*C. sempervirens*)

The Spell

Mix together the Himalayan salts and the bicarbonate of soda in the glass bowl. While stirring, say:

Ground and release, earth and peace.

Then add the Rose petals and say:

Love has come, now softly part.

Add the essential oils, mix well and say:

Find me a path of peace and of love,

Take me from here to something better thereof.

Decant into the jar and store in a cool dry place for about a month.

To use, simply tip the entire contents into a running bath, set up your image of the Tuscan landscape in front of you and enjoy a relaxing bath.

The Ancient Greeks and Romans called the Cypress 'the mourning tree' and planted it in graveyards and in front of homes when someone within had died, as they considered the tree sacred to the gods of the underworld.

The Cypress is also considered a symbol of resurrection and healing and so is perfect for magick and spells that require these energies. Traditionally a branch is cut from a Cypress tree very slowly, taking three months, and then this can create a healing wand. Pass over afflicted areas and cleanse by dipping the end in a flame after each use.

Pear Tree Regain Harmony Spell

Originating as a hybrid in western Asia over 2000 years ago, the Pear has been cultivated for hundreds of years, giving it a wide natural distribution throughout Europe. Such has been the popularity and extensive breeding of the Pear, it is impossible to discern what the Pear originally looked like.

Pears offer comfort, harmony, affection and balance and so are a lovely base for this peace-bringing drink. Share with those you may be experiencing some disquiet with to bring emotions and minds back into a more harmonious balance.

Timings
Waning Moon, Wednesday, Dusk

Find and Gather
» 1 cup of boiling water
» ¾ cup of caster (*superfine*) sugar
» 1 cup of fresh Lemon juice (*Citrus × limon*)
» 4 cups of cold sparkling water
» a large glass jug (*to store lemonade in fridge*)
» 3 ripe Pears (*Pyrus communis*)

The Spell

Mix together the boiling water and sugar and stir until dissolved.

Remove from heat and let cool completely. Pour into the jug. Add Lemon juice and cold sparkling water to the sugar mix and say:

Sweet and sour,

Mix and flow,

Bring harmony now,

With those that I know.

Slice the Pears, add to the jug and say:

Pears, in you go,

Balance and harmony be.

Use immediately, serving in beautiful tumblers full of ice cubes. If you wish to keep longer, omit the sparkling water and store in the fridge for up to three days, adding sparkling water when serving or substitute still for sparkling water.

If you dream of Pears, it is a very good omen and means great riches are coming your way. Should you be single, it indicates you will marry above your current socio-economic situation and should the Pears be cooked, such as in a pie, business success is on its way to you.

In Switzerland a lovely tradition sees families planting an Apple tree to commemorate the birth of a boy and a Pear tree for a girl. The trees are well cared for as the health and wellbeing of the child is said to be linked to their tree.

White Willow Tree Healing Heartbreak Spell

Growing in water meadows and along waterways, the beautiful Willow has leaves that are covered with fine soft hairs. When the leaves are moved by the wind, the tree has a beautiful silvery appearance. White Willow is found throughout much of Europe and western Asia.

Willow helps comfort those who have lost love and gives hope for a healed heart tomorrow. Find a place outside that you find comforting to create this spell. You will need to find a few items that you love: for example, if you love gardening, perhaps you might add a gardening tool; if it is crystals, you could add your favourite ones; if it is art, perhaps a paintbrush.

Timings
Full Moon, Friday, Evening

Find and Gather
» a few items that you really love
» a white Rose (*Rosa* spp.)
» a tiny jar of honey
» a small glass of milk
» a lovely cupcake or biscuit
» a stick of White Willow (*Salix alba*) – any size

Plate IX.—The White Willow (*Salix alba*).

The Spell

Place your loved treasures upon the ground. Holding your white Rose, slowly walk around your treasures in a circle, in anti-clockwise direction, while gently loosening the petals and letting them drift to the earth. Repeat until all petals have released and your circle is formed:

Let heartbreak leave,

The tears of mine cease,

With each petal released.

Tip a tiny dash of honey into the milk. Sit and enjoy your milk and sweet treat while imagining your heart healing. You should also be open to messages and ideas that should come to help find avenues to heal. Then pick up your Willow stick, draw a big heart on the ground around your treasures and say:

Within my heart love,

The things that glow.

Within my heart,

The healing grows.

Let the petals and heart blow away on their own.

It is believed that simply sitting beneath a Willow tree will give rise to great inspiration and confer eloquence upon artists, writers, speakers, poets, actors, priests and musicians.

In China the Willow is considered a symbol of immortality because it can grow from the smallest cutting. It is also thought to be a very lucky plant and able to protect against harm, evil and illness.

Cherry Tree Love Reality Check Spell

Wild Cherry is the parent tree of most of the Cherries we enjoy today and is also used as the rootstock onto which many other of the Rosaceae family are grafted. It is the largest of Europe's native Cherry trees and has a natural distribution across the continent.

This spell will help you sort out your feelings for another. Is it lust? Love? Or something else? Cherries have been used for centuries in love spells to attempt to gain the affections of the one desired. In this spell we are harnessing the lusty powers of Cherries with their ability to weed out insincerity while learning/remembering life lessons.

Timings
Full Moon, Friday, Late Night

Find and Gather

» a Cherry (*Prunus avium*) with the stalk still attached – it is preferable to pluck the Cherry from the tree yourself if possible

» a beautiful plate

» a hair from your head

» a hair from your love interest

» a camera, pen and paper or your phone

The Spell

Stand before the fruit-laden Cherry tree or before a tree proxy
(see page 12) or an image of the tree and say:

Is it love or is it lust?

Is it real or is it dust?

Cherry tree ripe and filled with fruit,

Please tell me tonight and don't be too cute!

Pluck a Cherry, being careful to leave the stalk on.

Place the Cherry on the plate and squish it down with
your finger until the skin splits to reveal the flesh. Lay each
of your collected hairs across the Cherry and say:

Here we are,

Them and me,

So what is it, Cherry?

What do you think it will be?

Take a photo (or make a sketch) of your arrangement,
noting which hair belongs to whom. Leave overnight.

In the morning if both hairs remain, it's love. If both
are gone, then it's lust, and if only one remains? Well then,
the one that remains is more invested in the relationship
than the other. Not all is lost but you might want to rethink
things.

In the botanical name
for Cherry, 'avium'
means 'of the birds'
and is named for the
birds that love this
fruit. Some of its
common names hint
at this, such as Bird
Cherry and Hawk
Berry.

Cherries have always
been a popular
divination tree. The
number of years you
might live is said to
be revealed if you
run around a Cherry
tree in full fruit and
shake it. The number
of fallen Cherries will
indicate the number
of years you still have
left on earth.

Linden Tree Forgiveness Spell

Found naturally from Portugal to the Caucasus, this very long-lived tree (some have been found to be up to 2000 years old), is an indicator of ancient woodland. Sweetly perfumed yellow flowers and heart-shaped leaves make this a very attractive tree.

Linden trees work very closely with energies surrounding friendships, peace, justice and love and in this spell you will be harnessing these energies to assist you in asking for forgiveness and to convey that you are truly sorry.

Timings
Full Moon, Sunday, Evening or Morning

Find and Gather
» a tray
» a white cloth
» a white candle
» a candle holder
» boiling water
» a beautiful teapot
» dried Linden flowers (*Tilia cordata*) or Linden tea

- » 2 white, or predominantly white, teacups
- » a pot of organic honey
- » spoons
- » a white Rose (*Rosa* spp.) – optional
- » a clear quartz crystal – optional
- » a Linden stick to stir your tea with

The Spell

Set the tray with the white cloth. Place the candle in its holder on the tray and light it.

Add the boiling water to the teapot then place it, the dried Linden flowers, the teacups, the pot of honey and the spoons on the tray and take to where you will be drinking the tea. You might like to add a white Rose (to indicate peace and purity of action) and perhaps a clear quartz crystal (to boost the power of your intentions) to the setting.

Sit with the person you wish to ask forgiveness from and share a cup of tea. If this is not possible, set up tea for two and imagine them there with you then go through the spell as follows:

Add 1 teaspoon of Linden flowers for each cup of water in the teapot. When you put the flowers into the teapot, make sure you say you are sorry to the other person in some way. Sweeten the tea with honey if required and stir with the Linden stick.

The Linden tree is usually considered to be female in many customs and traditions. In Lithuania, men make sacrifices to an Oak tree deity whereas women make sacrifices to that of the Linden tree.

The flowers of the Linden tree are useful as a support for the ailments associated with respiratory conditions including colds and flu. All parts of a Linden tree are edible – the leaves, bark, sap and the seeds along with the flowers.

Hawthorn Tree Strengthen Love Spell

*Found in many parts of the world, these trees have proved to be extremely
adaptable and tenacious. They cope with heavy pollution in cities, salt-
spray in rugged coastal areas and very low temperatures. Because of this,
and their beautiful form, flowers and fruit (known as haws), they are
popular garden and street trees.*

*This is a recipe to share and strengthen a couple's love for each other.
A good spell to do when there have been challenging times in your
relationship and you are in rebuilding mode. Hawthorn is included because
it provides balance and purification. Hawthorn also protects hearts, offers
hope and is symbolic of a sacred union. If you have no access to Hawthorn
you could substitute any other edible red fruit, but bring Hawthorn into
your magickal working through imagery.*

Timings
Full Moon, Monday, Morning/Midday

Find and Gather

» 1 kg (*2.2 lb*) ripe Hawthorn haws (*Crataegus
monogyna*)

» a towel

» water (*as needed*)

» 2 saucepans (*1 large*)

» a sieve

- » a masher or spoon
- » sugar (*as needed*)
- » a sugar thermometer
- » sterilised jars with lids

The Spell

Remove the stalks from the haws by rolling them in the towel and say:

Away with past and what has divided,
Strengthen our love with what is now decided.

Wash the haws very well, picking out any that are spoiled. Place in the large saucepan and add enough water to cover. Cook until they are very soft.

Strain through a sieve into a large bowl, pressing the haws with a masher or spoon to extract as much liquid as possible. Discard the haw pulp and seeds.

Pour the resulting liquid into a saucepan and add 1 cup of sugar for each cup of liquid. Bring to the boil, stirring to dissolve sugar. Continue to boil until the setting point is reached: 105°C (220°F).

Pour into warm sterilised bottles and seal. Store in a cool, dry place for up to 12 months. Refrigerate once opened and use within two weeks.

When using, spread a little on a sweet biscuit or cake to share and say:

Strengthening hearts,
Together we fare.
Let the challenge scars heal now,
And our love be given new care.

Other types of Hawthorn (*Crataegus* spp.) are also edible and can be used in this jelly. Check local guides as to their availability. Note the seeds are not edible as they contain small amounts of cyanide, much like apple seeds, so always discard.

Traditionally, winter is considered over when the Hawthorn flowers. This is probably why dreaming of Hawthorn when single means a new lover is assured pretty much immediately!

Apple Tree Love Spell

The Apple we are all familiar with comes from a tree that was originally from Central Asia where the wild trees are still found today. Humans have been planting Apple trees across the world for centuries. They have found their way from Asia through Europe and on to North America and beyond and have inspired myths and folklore.

This spell creates an old-fashioned Apple shampoo that will surround you with positive love energies to attract the right love for you. It will also help you see yourself in a positive light and love yourself more! Apple is used in this spell because it helps purify emotions, is an excellent self-care supporter and is symbolic of fertility, sensuality and love in general.

Timings
Full Moon, Friday, Morning

Find and Gather
» about 4–6 Apples (*Malus pumila*)
» a juicer

- » a large glass or ceramic bowl
- » 1 cup of distilled water
- » ¼ cup liquid Castile soap
- » 8 drops of Rose essential oil (*Rosa* spp.)
- » a wooden spoon
- » a fine strainer
- » a beautiful glass bottle with lid
- » a funnel (*optional*)

The Spell

Juice the Apples until you have 1 cup of juice. (You can substitute purchased Apple juice but make sure it is fresh pressed/juiced with no additives.) Pour into the bowl and then add the distilled water. Add the Castile soap and the Rose essential oil, stir well and say:

> *Rose oil, Apple tree,*
>
> *Together for me,*
>
> *A love that is true,*
>
> *A love that is right,*
>
> *Breathe love through my hair,*
>
> *Bring love's heart delight.*

Strain into the glass bottle, store out of direct sunlight and use within six weeks. To use: shake well and use as you would your regular shampoo.

If you would like to see a unicorn, it is said your best chance is to visit an orchard early on a misty spring morning, as they make their homes beneath Apple trees.

To find out if the one you desire loves you, throw an Apple pip (*seed*) onto a fire. You can say: 'If you love me pop and fly, if you do not lay and die.' If it pops, your love is returned, if it does not then they do not feel the same about you.

Sweet Orange Tree Friendship Spell

*Found growing naturally in China and naturalised in many parts
of the world, the sweet Orange is an important commercial crop.
Sweet Orange is also grown by home gardeners as an ornamental tree
as well as for its fruit.*

*This is a sparkling treat to share with friends to strengthen bonds,
heal rifts and encourage warmth and clear communication. Orange is
the base of the spell because it raises the energies of friendship, joy,
enthusiasm and bonds. The sharing of food and drink is a bonding
experience that humans have engaged in since time began so it makes
the perfect format for any friendship spell.*

Timings
Waxing Moon, Friday, Midday/Evening

Find and Gather

- » 12 Oranges (*Citrus sinensis*)
- » a juicer (*hand or electric*)
- » a beautiful clear glass/crystal jug
- » 1 bottle of champagne/sparkling wine or sparkling water
- » 3 teaspoons of Orange Blossom water
- » a wooden spoon
- » gorgeous glasses for you and your friends

The Spell

Juice the Oranges and add the jug and say:

> *Sweet Orange tree,*
>
> *Your fruit before me,*
>
> *Fallen from up high,*
>
> *Bring the joy from the sky.*

Pour in the champagne/sparkling wine or sparkling water and (using the version that suits) say:

> *Joyful wine (or water),*
>
> *Sparkle and dance,*
>
> *When friends gather round,*
>
> *Our bonds to be grown.*

Drop in the Orange Blossom water and stir with the wooden spoon while saying three times:

> *Flowers grow friendships.*

Pour into the glasses and serve.

Wine features in many old spells that you may come across. Orange juice itself has always been considered a perfect substitute for any alcoholic beverage called for in spells and ritual work.

Don't throw away Orange peel. Added to a bath, it can make you more attractive to those you may have a romantic interest in. Carrying it in your wallet or purse with an Orange pip can help attract wealth.

TREE SPELLS FOR
CHANGE AND
EMPOWERMENT

Eastern Cottonwood Tree Communication Spell

The hybridisation of the Black Poplar (Populus nigra) *and this tree, the Eastern Cottonwood, has produced the extensively planted and well-known P. x canadensis. The Eastern Cottonwood is found naturally from the eastern Rocky Mountains from Quebec through to Texas.*

Eastern Cottonwood is suggested for this spell because it assists with the opening of communication channels. These types of spells are helpful in times when you feel you are not being clearly heard by another person or group and while you cannot energetically change their opinion, you can raise energy to ensure you are better understood.

Timings
Full Moon, Wednesday, Dusk

Find and Gather

» a blue tablecloth or scarf
» 4 leaves from an Eastern Cottonwood tree (*P. deltoides*)
» 2 bells
» pen and paper
» a clear vase
» a small beautiful bottle with airtight top

- » water
- » glycerin

The Spell

Lay the cloth out neatly and place the leaves in a line on the cloth. At either end of the line, place a bell. Take the pen and paper and write what it is that you need to be understood. Ring the first bell, then say:

Hear these words,

And the things that I mean.

Then read what you have written.

Ring the second bell and say:

Make no mistake,

To take them to thee.

Fill your vase with the water and place the leaves in it. Place the vase on top of the paper you wrote on and put outside in the sunlight for a day.

Add water from the vase to your bottle till three-quarters full then add one-quarter glycerin. Whenever you wish your message to be heard, ring a bell and shake your bottle.

The distinctively triangular leaves is why this tree bears the botanical name *'deltoides'*, meaning 'triangular-shaped'.

Sacred to many Native American peoples, the Cottonwood is often thought of as a symbol of the sun and to some it symbolises the afterlife. The Hidatsa believe that by approaching with great respect and then standing in the shade of a Cottonwood you could have questions answered and be given insight and solutions to your problems.

Bay Laurel Tree Success Spell

Native to areas throughout the Mediterranean, the Bay Laurel was used by the Ancient Greeks to create wreaths to crown their sporting champions. The fragrant leaves are also used in cooking as an aromatic.

Bay leaves are used in this spell to raise the energy of victory and success that Bay Laurel shares. This tree symbolises immortality and provides protection from disease, misadventure and even witchcraft. In this spell you will be creating a headband decorated with Bay Laurel leaves. It is preferable that you carefully stitch them to the headband and focus on your success, but you can glue on the leaves using a cool-temperature glue gun.

Laurus.

Timings
Waxing Moon, Thursday, Daytime

Find and Gather
» fresh Bay Laurel leaves (*Laurus nobilis*) – at least 12
» a soft fabric headband
» thick needle and thread

» pen and paper

The Spell

Sit in a sunny and bright spot and carefully sew your Bay Laurel leaves onto your headband in a straight line so that the leaves circle the band. Use two or three large straight stitches and overlap the next leaf slightly. After each leaf is secured, say:

> Leaf of the circle,
>
> Take me on high with you too,
>
> Together may victory,
>
> Come swift and come true.

Once your wreath is complete, place it on your head, then take out the pen and paper and write down your success goals. Stand and read them out loud. Put the sheet of paper somewhere high in your home and place the Bay Laurel headband upon it.

The term 'poet laureate' comes to us from the Ancient Greek practice of also adorning acclaimed poets with fruiting branches of the Bay Laurel formed into wreaths.

If you feel you are going into a situation that may cause you to have bad luck or if you think you have bad luck at the moment, then try holding a Bay leaf under your tongue. Bay Laurel is considered to be a strong purification tree and along with breaking bad luck it is used in exorcisms and in cleansing rituals, mostly burned.

Magnolia Tree Legacy Protection Spell

Introduced to Europe in the 1700s, the Magnoliaceae family has 12 genera and over 200 species with many cultivars. These well-loved flowering trees have a native distribution across North America and Asia.

If you are creating anything that you consider to be a legacy, this is a strong and important spell that you can do to protect it. This can be anything that you envision will stay in your family or to be of continued benefit to others long-term, for example a body of work, a business, a family history record, or property. Magnolia is the tree selected to assist as it is a wisdom-keeper itself, a very strong protector against negative and harmful energies and a provider of great strength.

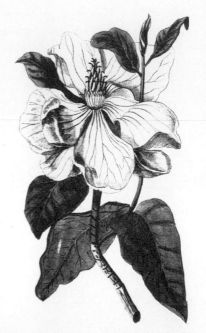

Timings
New Moon, Saturday, Late Night

Find and Gather
» a small branch of a Magnolia tree
   (*Magnolia* spp.) – any size
» secateurs
» an offering
» water
» a white fabric ribbon

The Spell

Magnolia trees seldom shed branches, but they do sometimes need pruning. You will need to respectfully harvest a branch for your spell. To do this, look carefully at the tree to select a branch that suits you and that feels ready to be harvested. Only take one. Your offering should be something biodegradable, perhaps a special small cake or biscuit you have made.

Once you have cut the branch with your secateurs, put your hand over the cut limb tightly and say:

Thank you wise tree,

I honour and respect thee.

Pour the water at the base of the tree and say:

May you never be thirsty.

Place your offering at the base of the tree and say:

May you have all that you need.

Tie the white ribbon where you cut your branch from and say:

My legacy grows and my legacy will be,

Protect and guide with love, oh great mighty tree.

Place the branch above the front door of where your legacy is. This could be your home or your business.

To ensure a lover stays true to you, place a Magnolia shoot under the bed. They will always then be faithful. To keep a business partner honest and loyal, place a Magnolia shoot under their desk or work area.

Magnolia have long been considered a female tree, of being a vessel of goddess energy and are symbolic of motherhood and feminine strength. This is perhaps due to its flower, which is a beautiful cup-like pink or white blossom.

Spindle Tree Shadow Self Spell

The Spindle tree is found throughout Europe. It grows along the edges of forests and hedgerows, creating a beautiful autumn display each year with the turning of its leaves from a pale green first to purple-red, then yellow, and striking red and orange fruit.

Spindle tree is the base of this spell as it is considered a tree that can unveil hidden knowledge, destiny and wisdom but also because it helps people examine their shadow self and understand how it may be impacting their lives.

Euonymus.

Timings
Dark Moon, Saturday, Midnight/Late Night

Find and Gather
» a small piece of Spindle wood (*Euonymus europaeus*)
» a piece of string about 15 centimetres (6 inches) long
» a pen/pencil and a sheet of paper – at least A3 size
» matches
» a fireplace or heat-proof dish

The Spell

You may like to carve the Spindle into a pendulum shape if you have the skill.

On the sheet of paper draw a circle as large as will fit. On the outside of the circle, equally spaced around it, write down all the shadow aspects of yourself. Be honest.

Tie the string to the Spindle wood and then hold the Spindle above the sheet of paper and say out loud what your challenges are. Let the Spindle spin and move as it will. Watch where it goes and what words it is pulled towards as these will be the shadow aspects of yourself that are most affecting your challenge. You might find some solutions or insights into how you can gain control or at least work a little better with your situation.

Once you have finished, burn the paper completely.

The Spindle tree was known as 'skewer wood' in Victorian times due to the practice of using its wood to make skewers. It has also been used to create spindles, clothes pegs and charcoal.

The tool of the Greek Fates that helped create the destiny of each human was a spindle made from the wood of the Spindle tree. They would spin a thread that represented the life, measure it and cut it.

White Poplar Tree Guidance Spell

The White Poplar is native to western Asia, North Africa and Europe. A very hardy tree, it is often used as a roadside city tree because it tolerates pollution well. White Poplars are fast-growing and have white downy hairs on the underside of their leaves and covering their shoots. On windy days this gives the impression that the tree is covered in silver.

White Poplar is used in this guidance spell as it helps find guidance and to calm fears you may have in moving forward. You will be creating a simple dance ribbon for this spell and using it much the same way gymnasts do, by twirling it through the air around you – and yes, you can dance!

Timings
New Moon, Monday, Late Night

Find and Gather
» a White Poplar stick or small branch (*Populus alba*)
» a 4-metre (*13-foot*) white ribbon

The Spell
Tie the ribbon to one end of the stick. Take this outside and think about the thing you are seeking guidance with. Walk around (or dance!), twirling the ribbon through the air as you do. When it feels right,

safely toss the stick in the air and let the ribbon and stick fall where they may.

Examine the patterns you see in the ribbon and the way the stick is lying. You might like to take a photo for reference so you can look at it again, but you really should try to tune into the messages before you.

Look out for letters, numbers, crosses, arrows or circles as they can indicate very definite answers. You may like to see if there are shapes of animals, objects and so on, as well, as these will all have meanings. Look up a tea-leaf reading dictionary for interpretations. Dream guides and magickal correspondences lists will also be helpful.

You could make a mini version of this divination dance stick by using a small White Poplar twig and thinner 'baby' ribbon cut to your desired length. Simply twirl in the air and let it land on a table.

Due to the way its leaves tremble in the slightest breeze, White Poplar is often regarded as a folklore remedy or an ingredient of magickal spells to cure diseases with the symptom of trembling, such as palsy. The trees also carry the common names of 'quivering tree', 'quaking tree' and 'trembling tree'.

According to Roman legend, Hercules wove a crown of Poplar leaves to protect himself from the flames of the Underworld on his journey there. They became scorched from the heat on the topside but turned light from the reflection of Hercules's face, as it possessed a god-like radiance.

Dragon's Blood Tree Hex Breaker Spell

The Dragon's Blood Tree is probably most noted for the incense made from its distinctive red resin but has an equally interesting appearance. This native to the Socotra Archipelago in Yemen has an overall structure similar to that of an open umbrella.

The combination of fire and ice in this hex-breaker is a very final way to resolve the issue. Using Dragon's Blood will give you complete protection, which is vital when going into the energies of a hex in order to break it. It also gives you courage when going into battle or facing challenges and it will increase your personal power.

Timings
Waning Moon, Tuesday, Midnight

Find and Gather
» pen and small piece of paper
» a heat-proof dish
» matches
» a small plastic container
» water
» a stick of Dragon's Blood incense or a few small pieces of resin (*Dracaena cinnabari*)

The Spell

Write down the hex as you believe it to be on the piece of paper. Burn it in the heat-proof dish and say:

Fire dissolve the words against me,

Fire break the hex that has been.

Let the ashes cool completely then place them in your plastic container. Pour in enough water to cover the ashes and stir with the Dragon's Blood incense stick. Break the stick up and throw it into the container. Place in the freezer. As you do, say:

Frozen you are,

No longer you move.

Be gone from my life,

And never return.

Leave for 90 days and then bury off your property.

You can add Dragon's Blood resin or incense or in fact any botanical part to your spellwork for a turbo boost. This would be very helpful if you are redoing a spell because the first time it wasn't as affective as you had hoped.

Dragon's Blood can be used to create a red ink that is very powerful when used for writing spellwork. Mix 1 part powdered Dragon's Blood resin to one part Arabic gum and then 10–15 parts alcohol (*depending on consistency*).

Mangrove Tree Opportunity Spell

Growing in coastal areas, in salt or brackish water, Mangrove trees are found throughout the world in tropical and subtropical regions. They offer a home for young organisms and some protection against coastal erosion. Although there are many different types of trees and plants that can grow within the Mangrove forest, there are only a few that are actual 'Mangrove trees' and they are found in the plant family Rhizophoraceae.

The use of Mangrove tree in this spell is to tap into the energies of opportunity, adaptability, availability and the ability to put things to best use. If you do live near Mangroves then by all means go to the forest, but you will still need to do this spell the way it is set out. It relies on you imitating a Mangrove tree yourself.

Timings
Full Moon/Waxing Moon, Thursday, Daytime

Find and Gather
» a blue cup or jug
» a jar with lid
» a handful of small seashells/sand/pebbles
» salt

The Spell

Take yourself to the seaside or a Mangrove forest if lucky enough to be near. If neither is available to you then a river, dam, stream or lake will do and if no waterway is available to you at all, stand in a basin or bath. You will then need enough water to cover your feet.

Standing with your feet covered in water and your toes splayed open say:

I stand as a Mangrove,
Firm here on the shore
Water comes in,
Tide pulls you out,
Within there lies chances,
Here, there, all about.

Scoop up a cupful of water and place in the jar. If possible, add a handful of small seashells/sand/pebbles to the water and if not near salt water, a good dash of salt. Seal and take home. Whenever you want new opportunities or for something to go your way, shake the jar and ask it:

Mangrove water,
Move for me now,
Water comes in,
Tide pulls you out,
Within there lies chances,
Here, there, all about.

To survive, Mangrove trees are not only tolerant of salt but also have a complex root system to withstand waves and tides. They are also able to live with very low oxygen supplies when growing in waterlogged mud.

Mangroves stand between two worlds, the sea and the land, and so can be helpful in any magickal work that requires two aspects of something to be balanced, changed or explored. Decisions especially around emotions (*water*) and the physical (*earth*) can benefit.

Elder Tree Evolution Spell

The Elder is actually a shrub, not a tree, but is included in this collection as it is often referred to as a tree in magickal traditions. Native to Europe and North America, it is also widely known as Elderberry. The flowers are used to make cordial and other drinks while the berries are used for syrup and jelly, and both are used for wine.

Elderflowers are used in this spell because flowers in general symbolise evolution and growth as they are the reproductive parts of a plant. If you use the flowers, you must cook them as they are toxic if consumed raw. Elder trees instil inner strength, self-esteem and courage. They will boost your vigour, impart good luck and nurture progress while giving you the fortitude to carry on. This spell works very well for those creating vision boards.

Timings
Waxing Moon, Saturday, Daytime

Find and Gather
- » your favourite cupcake recipe and ingredients
- » a handful of Elderflowers (*Sambucus nigra*) — spell can be completed without these
- » elderflower cordial

- » 2 beautiful glasses, one larger and grander than the other
- » sparkling water
- » your journal, diary or vision board

The Spell

Make a cupcake batter, then mix the elderflowers into the batter and say:

> *Elder wise,*
> *Elder strong,*
> *Help me go from here,*
> *To evolve where I long.*

Bake your cupcakes and then set up a beautiful table with the glasses, sparkling water, elderflower cordial and a cupcake and have your diary/journal/vision board before you.

Place a dash of elderflower cordial in the smaller glass and fill with sparkling water. Pour this into the other glass and say:

> *Today I stand here,*
> *Tomorrow I rise,*
> *Evolving with passion,*
> *Becoming the wise.*

Eat the cupcake and drink the elderflower water.

Elder is connected with the White Goddess in Pagan traditions and brings healing and comfort. Planting one in a garden or working field is thought to bring good luck and protection.

Growing an Elder tree in your garden will ensure that the mother Elder protects it and it is also thought that doing so will ensure that the gardener dies in their own bed. As it is also said that having this tree growing in your garden might discourage friends from visiting you, perhaps a 'welcome friends' spell would help!

Pine Tree Increase Intuition Spell

Any conifer in the Pinus genus is considered a pine tree. They are long-living trees with age ranges recorded from 100 to more than 1000 years. Native to the Northern Hemisphere and small tropical areas of the Southern Hemisphere, they are found in a vast range of climates from sea level to 5200 metres (17,100 feet). These include rainforests, deserts and the tropics.

Pine will open up paths between worlds, especially above and below the earth. This tree also helps strengthen faith, imparts longevity and keeps things true. For this spell, a traditional Witch Bottle will be made. Also known as Spell Bottles, they have been in use since at least the early 17th century in the UK and USA. This is a way of capturing energies to be used time and again and so they must be created with great care.

Timings
New Moon, Monday, Late Night

Find and Gather
» a purple candle
» a candle holder
» matches
» a small handful of dried Pine needles (*Pinus* spp.)
» a beautiful clear bottle and seal

» any small crystals that you are drawn to

» water

» a purple ribbon

The Spell

Set the candle in the candle holder and light. Add your Pine needles to the bottle and then say:

Above and below,

Connect and inspire,

Intuition be sharp,

And alive in the fire.

Hold your bottle high above the flame as you say the last line.

Add the crystals and fill with water, then seal the bottle and tie the purple ribbon around the neck. Whenever you are seeking clearer intuition, simply shake your bottle then sit quietly and watch the contents completely settle. You should receive thoughts that will help you and you will naturally strengthen your intuitive powers.

The oldest living Pine tree can be found in California, USA. It is a Great Basin Bristlecone Pine (*P. longaeva*) that has been nicknamed 'Methuselah' and is around 4600 years old.

If you collect a Pine cone that still contains Pine nuts on Midsummer Day and then eat one of the nuts each day until finished, you are said to become invincible.

Ash Tree Magickal Empowerment Spell

The common Ash tree grows wild in Europe from the Pyrenees through to the Caucasus. All Ash trees can be found growing in the temperate areas of the world but in particular Europe, Asia and North America.

Ash is selected as it symbolises power and mastery and will also increase psychic awareness. This spell requires the creation of a small and very simple doll, traditionally called a 'poppet', that is going to contain your spell and be something you can carry with you if needed.

Timings
Full Moon, Sunday, Midday

Find and Gather
» pins
» 2 pieces of red fabric
» a black felt-tip pen
» scissors
» a needle
» red thread
» shavings of pieces of Ash tree bark (*Fraxinus excelsior*)
» a clear quartz crystal

The Spell

Pin fabric pieces together. With the black felt-tip pen, draw a simple human figure on the top piece. Cut out the figure. Sew the pieces together, leaving a small opening at the top of the head.

Fill the doll with the Ash tree bark and say:

Ash tree of power,

Of magick and might,

I call on your gifts,

With a promise to do right.

Add the crystal and sew up the opening. You can now carry this with you when you want a boost in magickal power, use it during other spells and rituals or leave it in places to inspire magick.

Ash trees grow well in soils that are calcareous limestone-based. The timber is very strong, impact-resistant and durable so has been used to create tools and ladders as well as horse-drawn coaches.

You can also boost your psychic abilities by placing an Ash leaf under your pillow at night. You should have prophetic dreams so be sure to keep a dream journal nearby.

Brig o' Doon

TREE SPELLS
FOR PURPOSE
AND PATHS

Spruce Tree Awaken My Passion Spell

Spruces grow in the colder regions of the Northern Hemisphere. They are pyramid-shaped trees and although they look similar to Fir trees, you can identify Spruces by the peg-like stump on each needle where it's attached to the twig.

Spruce is used to create this anointing oil. Use it daily to find and grow your life passion. Spruce instils boldness and passion and will help you let go of self-pity and any weakness that does you no good. This spell will help with those who may be finding it hard to define their purpose or fire up their passion, or perhaps feel they have lost their way a little.

Timings
Full Moon, Sunday, Midday

Find and Gather
» a red cloth
» a clear glass or crystal bowl
» a fire agate crystal
» 1 cup of sweet Almond oil
» 11 drops of Spruce essential oil (*Picea* spp.)
» a beautiful sterilised bottle
» organic cotton wool pads or balls

The Spell

Spruce oil is safe for most people to use on their skin but you should still allergy-test yourself first. If you are anointing surfaces with the oil, please do a test somewhere inconspicuous first.

In the place in your home which is most used by you, lay out your red cloth and place the bowl upon it. Place the fire agate crystal in the bowl, then gently pour in the Almond oil and say three times:

Oil of Spruce,

Stone of fire,

Passion be found,

Then take me higher.

Pour the oil into the bottle. You can now help enliven your passion and find your purpose by lightly anointing the doorways of each room of your home/workspace with the oil or by placing a cotton pad/ball on a dish somewhere in each room. Place the fire agate near to the place where you work/create or generally are in your home or place of business.

The Norway Spruce (*P. abies*) is the traditional Christmas tree of most European countries. It is also the tree from which timber is used to create the bodies of many stringed instruments including the violin.

Most trees in the Northern Hemisphere shed their leaves during the colder months of the year so it was believed that the trees that held their leaves, like the Spruce, had power over death because they harboured good and pure spirits. Spruce branches and later the trees themselves were brought into homes in the winter to afford the same protection.

Hickory Tree Personal Path Spell

A member of the Juglandaceae (Walnut) family, the Hickory tree has large aromatic leaves and is deciduous. It's native to North America, Mexico, China and Indochina. Hickory and Oak are the dominant trees of the hardwood forests of North America.

Hickory is used here because it will impart patience, flexibility and strength. This spell creates a magickal floor wash. These have been used since we have had floors. It makes sense that the place where we meet the earth and that we place our feet upon should be energetically cleansed and empowered. The addition of Orange Blossom to your floor wash water will effectively and positively lift your energy.

Timings
Waxing Moon, Thursday, Dusk/Twilight

Find and Gather

» ½ bucket water
» ½ cup Hickory leaves (*Carya* spp.)
» ¼ cup Orange Blossom water
» a bucket
» a mop

The Spell

Open all the windows and doors of your home. Pour the water into a clean bucket then toss in your Hickory leaves. Put the mop in, stir in a clockwise direction and say:

Hickory strong, patient and true,

Find me a path that is right and is true.

Stir in your Orange Blossom water and say:

Orange tree sweet,

Happy and bright,

Keep me uplifted,

True, steady and right.

Wash over the floor and as you do, work your way towards the front door. Go outside and throw the remaining water and the leaves on your front path.

If you do not have hard floors, you can create a mist with a smaller amount of water and Orange Blossom water in a misting bottle. Place a chopped up Hickory leaf inside and then spray on your floors.

Hickory is an exceptionally strong timber and is used to craft tools, walking sticks, sporting clubs and sticks, paddles and furniture. Having almost the strength of steel and yet a considerable amount of flexibility led the Native Americans to use it to make their bows.

You can predict the weather by looking at Hickory nuts. The thickness indicates what the coming winter will have in store. The thicker the shell, the more challenging the season will be for everyone.

Yew Tree Rebirth Spell

Found in North America, Asia and Europe, the Yew grows mostly in the middle latitudes, but a few are found in tropical highlands. Although they are poisonous, they are still favoured as a decorative garden tree.

The inclusion of Yew in this spell must be done carefully as it is highly poisonous. It is better to be in presence of the actual tree and create a ritual to capture the energy, however there are flower essences based on Yew that could be substituted for being in the presence of the tree.

Timings
Full Moon, Sunday, Morning

Find and Gather
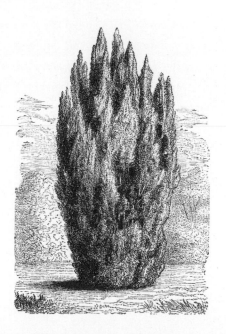

» a beautiful wooden box
» a small mirror which will fit in the bottom of the box
» a Yew tree (*Taxus baccata*)
» a piece of green coloured silk
» 2 teaspoons of dried Sacred Blue Lily flowers (*Nymphaea caerulea*)
» matches
» a fire or heat-proof dish
» 9 small clear quartz crystal points

The Spell

Take out the mirror and capture the image of the Yew tree in it. Place the green cloth loosely in the box, then the mirror, and say:

Time has come for me to let go,
Yew tree now is the time,
I do know.

Place the Sacred Blue Lily flowers in the dish and light or toss into the fire and say:

Listen tree, day and night,
When I next open this box,
A new birth sees the light.

Place the crystals around in the box and as you add each, say:

Protect and empower,
The new life begun,
May it strengthen and thrive,
All its days in the sun.

Take the box home and when you are ready to end something in your life and start anew, open the box. Leave it so for 7 days and then bury it under the Yew tree or another strong young (but long-lived) tree.

The Yew tree is sacred to the Goddess Hecate. Ancient Romans would adorn black bulls with Yew branches and leaves and then sacrifice them to Hecate at Saturnalia to ensure a tolerable winter. It was thought that ghosts would feed on the bull and not the remaining herd.

To dream of Yew trees can mean an escape from a very serious accident or it can mean the passing of a friend from illness.

Mesquite Tree Awaken Creativity Spell

Mesquites are native to the south-western United States and Mexico (except Creeping Mesquite, which is from Argentina). Mesquite is a legume and is one of the very few sources of fixed nitrogen in the desert environments in which it grows.

Mesquite is included in this creativity opening spell as it has a natural energy-warming ability, inspires healing and will encourage abundance. I find my creativity is bound by my emotions so bringing the power of fire into the emotional element of water should help balance things. This water can be used any time you would like to stimulate creativity. If it is raining, collect rainwater for an added magickal boost.

Timings
Waxing Moon, Friday, Evening

Find and Gather
» a beautiful white cloth
» a large, beautiful bowl
» pure water
» a fire
» a handful of Mesquite wood (*Prosopis* spp.)
» a mirror
» a special bottle

The Spell

Find a place outside where you can see the moon. Lay the white cloth out on the ground and say:

Gently touched with cloth of white,

Ground in Earth for magick tonight.

Set the bowl upon the cloth. Pour in the pure water and say:

Water of heart, of love and of care,

Support and bring comfort to all that is there.

Toss your Mesquite wood into the fire and say:

Tree of warmth,

Inspiration bright,

Creativity open,

For me from this night.

Taking the mirror, angle it so you catch the reflection of the moon and bounce it into the bowl of water. Tend the fire but let it burn out. Leave the bowl out for the night. The next morning, scoop a little of the Mesquite ash into the bottle and fill with the water. Use it sparingly as you would a flower essence mist by spritzing in the air when you need a creativity boost.

Mesquite is the most common tree and shrub of the southwestern United States. It has been described as a gift from heaven by the early settlers, who used it as a primary food source when stocks ran out. The beans can be eaten, made into a flour and also roasted as a substitute for coffee.

To many of the Native American peoples, Mesquite is regarded as a Tree of Life. This is probably due to all parts of these hardy desert plants being useful.

Aspen Tree Overcome Obstacles Spell

Native to North America, Aspens live in areas of colder weather and particularly cool summers. Most Aspens grow in large colonies, coming from a single seedling, and then spread by means of root suckers.

Aspen trees connect with the yin and the yang of anything they are in the presence of. They represent the duality of a situation so that you are aware of what has been and what may be possible. Aspen will still and calm fears, inspire trust in love and will also work to provide opportunities for success and abundance so that you can move forward. This is a very simple spell but still very powerful. You will be jumping a stick of Aspen to jump your obstacle.

Timings
New Moon, Tuesday, Twilight

Find and Gather
» 2 bricks (*or other objects to raise each end of the stick slightly*)
» a stick or branch of Aspen (*Populus tremula, P. tremuloides.*) at least ½ metre (*20 inches*) long
» a pen and paper
» 2 red candles
» 2 candle holders
» matches
» a heat-proof dish

The Spell

Set the bricks on the ground, spaced out so that you can rest an end of the Aspen stick on each. The Aspen stick only has to be raised slightly off the ground so you can step over it. Take your paper and write down your obstacle. Put a candle holder with a red candle in it on the ground at each end of the Aspen stick. Make sure they are a safe distance away, so you do not set your clothing on fire while preforming this spell.

Light each candle and say:

With fire I fight and burn away what is stopping me.

Stand on one side of your stick, holding the paper, and say:

These obstacles are ashes on the side that I leave.

Walk over to a candle and light the paper, dropping it into the heat-proof dish to burn.

Step or jump over the Aspen stick and say:

A new path I've taken,

A new start begun,

May the blocks that have barred me,

Be forever now done.

Clap your hands loudly to send the energy forward. Bury all your ingredients except your holders, bricks and the tray under a tree.

Aspen trees are aligned with the New Moon and are considered the Virginal Goddess tree. Any magical ritual or spell cast at this time would be empowered by the addition of Aspen, so closely connected is this tree.

Known as the 'whispering tree', a messenger and also associated with the god Mercury, communication is another strong aspect of the Aspen. If you wish to increase your own powers of communication, place an Aspen leaf under your tongue.

Silver Fir Progress Spell

Native to the mountain regions of Europe, this is a popular Christmas tree in the north-east of North America and Canada. It can live for more than 30 years and this makes it the longest lived of the conifers.

Silver Fir is a wonderful tree to engage when you want to move your progress along a little faster. It also helps with checking in on how you are going, as it imparts great clarity in all things.

Timings
Waxing Moon, Wednesday, Daytime

Find and Gather
» a large bowl
» a watering can with a sprinkler head to mimic rain
» water
» Silver Fir essential oil (*Abies alba*)
» orange food colouring/dye
» a stick or twig of Silver Fir if possible – if not, any twig

The Spell

Place the bowl on a table in a quiet room. Using the watering can, fill it with water to about the halfway point and as you do, say:

Rain of the season,

Come down and now see,

How well I am doing,

And what I may need.

Add 8 drops of Silver Fir essential oil and say:

Tree of silver,

Guide my way.

Now add a small dash of the orange colouring, stir with the twig and say:

Empower my progress,

Make it faster and fresh,

Ensure each step that I take,

Is always the best.

This spell can also be used to divine ways for added success and progress by examining any patterns or symbols that you see in the water.

The Silver Fir is the tree of the Winter Solstice day and is also strongly aligned with the moon and the triple aspect of the Goddess. It is also sacred to Diana, Artemis, Osiris and Attis.

To farewell a friend who is leaving, a gift or a wearable talisman created from the pine cones of the Silver Fir will ensure good luck and safe journeys. Burning the needles of the tree around the bed of a newborn baby is said to similarly bless the child with a safe and lucky life journey.

Fig Tree Magickal Power Booster Spell

*Cultivated throughout the world in temperate regions for its fruit, the Fig
tree was originally from south-west Asia and the Middle East. This tree
has been cultivated since ancient times and can grow wild from sea level
to 1700 metres (5577 feet).*

*This is a spell which will have you creating a very easy Fig jam. Use it to
boost your spellcasting by taking a spoonful yourself or you could use it as
your offering to the trees that you are working with. Figs are aligned with
the energies of longevity, fertility, love.*

Timings
Full Moon, Sunday, Midday

Find and Gather

» 4 cups of sliced Figs (*Ficus carica*)
» 1½ cups of granulated sugar
» ¼ cup water
» ¼ cup lemon juice
» Pinch of salt
» a saucepan
» sterilised jars

The Spell
Place all ingredients in a saucepan and say:
Fig of abundance,

I honour your power,

Simmer here in my brew,

For just a wee hour.

Bring to a boil until sugar dissolves, stirring occasionally. Reduce heat and cook, continuing to stir occasionally. This should take between 40–60 minutes, depending on the Figs but the liquid should be thick and sticky. Remove from heat. Gently mash any large pieces of Figs with a fork.

As you mash, say:

The brew is done!

The magick released,

Now into my jars,

To safely keep!

Pour into warm jars, leaving a small space, and seal.

Let cool, then store jam in the refrigerator for up to two months.

The Bible does tell us that the forbidden fruit was an Apple, but these days botanists agree that it was more likely a Fig. Apples did not grow in the region described in the story of Genesis at that time, but the Fig did, and the attributes could align with the biblical story.

Fig leaves can be used for simple divination answers. Write your question on a fresh Fig leaf in pen. If the Fig leaf seems quick to dry out, then the answer is negative or not. If the leaf is slow to dry, then the answer is yes.

Silver Birch Tree Find Your Way Spell

One of the first trees to colonise northern Europe after the last ice age was the Silver Birch. This tree is one of the hardiest trees on earth: it can live through drought and withstand extreme cold. It seeds abundantly. This tree is included in this spell as the name is thought to have come to us from the Sanskrit word 'bhurg', meaning the continuous phases of life and describing the energies that Silver Birch imparts.

Timings
New Moon, Friday, Sunrise

Find and Gather
» a large map – can be of any place
» 4 candles – 1 of each colour: red, pink, white and blue
» holders for the candles
» matches
» 11 small Silver Birch sticks (*Betula pendula*) – similar in shape and size as 'pick-up-sticks'

The Spell

Set a protected space and place your map upon a flat surface.
Set the candles up at each corner of the map. Light each,
saying:

Red is for action that I might have to take,

Pink for the healing I am yet to make.

White is for that which I need to let go,

Blue for the things I am yet to know.

Hold your Silver Birch sticks over the middle of the map
and drop them, asking:

What do I need?

Where shall I go?

Tell me, Silver Birch, what it is I must know.

Look at where most of the sticks are pointing because this
will indicate what it is you need to do in order to find your
way at the moment.

Traditionally, babies' cradles were made from Birch as it was considered to be the most protective of all the woods when it came to children. Such a cradle would ensure no harm would come to the child. Birch leaves were also placed under the pillows of sick children and babies to give them the strength to shake off the illness.

Birch trees are used in some regions as a type of living May Pole during Beltane celebrations of the Pagan calendar. The bonfires are typically lit with Birch branches but are made from Oak.

Hemlock Tree Secret Reveal Spell

The Hemlock tree is a long-lived conifer found naturally in North America and Asia. It has earned its common name because the leaves, when crushed, smell very like the poisonous Hemlock plant (Conium maculatum) *but it is not related.*

Hemlock tree is used in this spell because it has the energies of transformation, revelation and offering assistance. Because it is rather easy to find small lower branches of Hemlock trees suitable to use as wands as they are, in this spell you will be crafting a wand that you can use forever to find the answers to secrets, unfold mysteries and even help you learn esoteric knowledge.

Timings
New Moon, Monday, Late Night

Find and Gather

» a small branch of a Hemlock tree
   (*Tsuga canadensis*) – sized to suit you
» a cup of Hemlock tree needles
» a cup of boiling water
» a teapot and 2 cups

The Spell
Clean and trim the branch as you like
and if you desire, carve or decorate it.

It is perfectly okay for you to leave the branch exactly as you found it, as it is to create something crafty. This is your wand, so do what feels right for you.

Set a lovely tea service for two, somewhere quiet in your home. Put your new Hemlock tree wand on the table behind one teacup, as if it were joining you for tea, which it is!

Crush the Hemlock needles in your hands and drop into the teapot, saying:

Hemlock tree,

Warm and unlock for me,

Secrets and answers,

Of mysteries deep.

Pour over the boiling water and let steep for 5 minutes. Pour a cup for you and your wand and ask the wand:

What is your name, my new wand friend?

You should give the wand the first name that pops into your head.

Drink your tea, take the wand outside, pour its cup over it and say:

insert name together we shall be,

I'll honour and protect,

My word you shall have

Of my utmost respect.

Use the wand by waving it over rituals, spells, books – anything that you are trying to decipher. Make sure you always ask the wand by name to help you and thank it.

The needles of the Hemlock tree are sometimes used to make a tea and perfume. The resin can be burned to produce a lovely incense that also imparts the energetic qualities of Hemlock tree.

Hemlock tree features in many Native America myths and stories and all seem to carry the message that the tree provides a refuge, a way of escape and as a solution to adversity.

Olive Tree Inner Peace Spell

The Olive is a small tree that grows naturally in the Mediterranean, the Arabian Peninsula, southern Asia and the Canary Islands. This tree produces the fruit, also called olive, that is a major agricultural crop of the Mediterranean region.

This spell creates a relaxing oil hair treatment that will impart the peaceful qualities of Olive tree to you all day long and give you beautifully shiny, healthy hair and a healthy scalp. Use as much as your hair will tolerate. Thick, dry or damaged hair will probably need the entire mixture while normal or oily hair will only require a small amount.

Timings
Waning Moon, Friday, Dusk/Late Night

Find and Gather
» a white cloth
» a white candle
» a candle holder
» matches
» a small bowl
» a sprig of Rosemary (*Rosmarinus officinalis*)
» 4 tablespoons of virgin Olive oil (*Olea europaea*)

» 4 drops of Rosemary essential oil (*Rosmarinus officinalis*)

» an Olive wood stick (*optional*) or a wooden spoon

The Spell

Lay out your white cloth and white candle and light it.

Into the bowl place the Rosemary, then pour over the Olive oil and set it before the candle.

Lift it up and say:

Tree of peace,

Of inner strength and harmony,

Surround me with your blessings.

Put the bowl down and add the drops of Rosemary essential oil, and with each, say:

Carry the blessings,

Remember the peace.

Stir with the Olive tree stick or a wooden spoon. With your hair dry, massage the oil mixture into your scalp and comb through your hair, right through to the ends. Wrap up your hair in a damp, warm towel and leave for 15–30 minutes. Wash and condition.

Olive has been used throughout time as an anointing oil and as lamp oil to provide light in holy temples. Olive oil also provides the base of 'Holy Oil'. This oil represents the wisdom of God. The other oils included are Myrrh, Galangal and Cinnamon.

To dream of eating Olives means that you are going to receive a really wonderful gift and could also rise in your status. If you dream of gathering Olives then the omen is very much in your favour for happiness, joy and peace.

OLD TREE IN BIRNAM WOOD.

TREE SPELLS
FOR THE EARTH
AND LIFE

A Tree Planting Spell

This spell is for any tree you plan on growing anywhere. It assists the tree to take root and thrive but also to send out energies to protect others of its kind and trees in general.

The offering that you will be gathering to put inside the jar must correspond with the characteristics of your tree. Research crystal correspondences to find suitable crystals, symbols, animals (so you can include their images), other plants and so on.

Timings
Full Moon, Monday, Morning

Find and Gather
» your tree
» gardening tools and supplies as suggested for your tree
» a lovely glass jar and lid
» offerings for your tree
» milk
» honey
» water

The Spell

When planting a tree, the usual rule is to dig a hole twice as deep and as wide as the pot your tree came out of, but check with the nursery for exact instructions. You will perhaps also need extra suitable soil, fertiliser, mulch and so on, and you will need to make sure the position you select is suitable for the tree.

Plant your tree and as you do, speak to it: encourage it to grow strong and tell it why you selected it, what you hope for it and give it promises of your commitment to its care.

Fill the jar with your offerings. Dig a hole nearby. Tell the tree why you selected these gifts, listing each, and then bury it near the tree and say:

> *If ever I am not here,*
> *These gifts will keep you company,*
> *I hope they remind you that you are loved,*
> *And respected in this place.*

Pour a little milk and honey on the ground around the tree and say:

> *May you never go thirsty or hungry,*
> *And may the good spirits of this place welcome you.*

Water the tree well.

Knocking on a wooden piece of furniture or object to counter any bad luck that might befall you once you mention something with negative possibilities comes from the ancient belief that Pagan gods lived inside trees. If you knocked on the tree you could awaken the gods and then ask for their assistance.

You should avoid planting very large or tall trees to the east or the north-east of your home as according to many traditions and to Feng Shui advice they will emit negative energies in such positions.

American Sycamore Gardener Success Spell

Sycamore is a common name which refers to many different types of trees across the world and across different genera. The American Sycamore is found naturally growing in eastern and central North America and north-eastern Mexico.

Use this spell when planting a new garden or a new bed or crop. It will ensure added protection of your plants and more vigorous growth. Moss agate is known as the 'gardener's crystal' or stone. It will not only increase your own gardening skills if worn, the crystal will also improve the growth of any plant if placed in the soil alongside it.

Timings
Full Moon/Waxing Moon, Thursday, Morning

Find and Gather

» 4 sticks fashioned from Sycamore branches or wood (*Platanus occidentalis*)
» a cup of milk
» 4 green moss agate crystals
» 4 leaves of American Sycamore
» 4 gold coins

The Spell

Mark out the corners of your garden space that you are creating the spell for. It could be the entire garden or block, a bed or a crop area.

Dip the end of each of the Sycamore sticks into the milk and say:

Blessed with milk,

Blessed with the life,

Go into the ground,

And make everything thrive.

Stake a stick firmly in the ground at each corner of your defined space. Wrap each green moss agate in a Sycamore leaf and push one down in the earth next to each stick. Push down a gold coin with each as well and say:

I pay thee well,

I pay thee true,

Now set about,

Do what you do.

Some Native American tribes consider Sycamores to be the ghosts of the forest, due to their twisted limbs. One story tells of a great chief who ruled over the evil spirits. He was angry with two of his tribe and so cast them down to earth. They crashed into a Sycamore tree, turning it twisted with their evil spirits.

In Ancient Egyptian times, Sycamore trees were considered to be the connectors between the lands of the living and the world of the dead. It was believed to be from the Sycamore tree that the sun was released each morning.

Palo Santo Tree Sacred Space Spell

The common name of this tree is Spanish for 'holy stick'. It is native to Mexico, Peru and Venezuela. Palo Santo is a member of the same family as Myrrh and Frankincense and is a favourite folk medicine for a variety of complaints.

Palo Santo is used in this spell because it is a powerful purifier and positive energy bringer. The wood enhances creativity, instils universal love and strengthens spiritual connections. It also helps create a sacred space for you to work within. The combination of making a tea and a mojo bag out of the same stick is an important step because the energy of the shared experience will strengthen the bond between self and space.

Timings
Full Moon, Sunday, Evening

Find and Gather
» a sharp knife
» 1 stick of Palo Santo heartwood (*Bursera graveolens*)
» a teapot
» 2 cups of boiling water
» a strainer
» a teacup

- » honey
- » a small mojo bag
- » string or ribbon

The Spell

With the sharp knife, very carefully shave off about 2 teaspoons of Palo Santo wood. Place 1 teaspoon in your teapot and pour in the boiling water. As you do, say:

Wood of Palo Santo,

Healer divine,

Clear this space and make sacred,

From now for all time.

Pour through a strainer into your teacup and sweeten with a little honey.

Put the other teaspoon of Palo Santo shavings into the mojo bag and say again:

Wood of Palo Santo,

Healer divine,

Clear this space and make sacred,

From now for all time.

Once you have finished your tea, use the string or ribbon to hang the mojo bag above the main entrance to your space.

The wood of Palo Santo will purify, remove negative energy and impart positive energy at the same time. This is a trait that not many other plants share. The smoke can also help people focus better and is a very powerful meditation supporter.

Palo Santo sticks that are of a yellow colour are from the female trees and those that are white are male. Both have the same qualities and uses but there are additional aspects you might like to consider in magickal work that is closely associated with gender.

Chestnut Tree Nature Regeneration Spell

Chestnuts are trees with edible nuts that are within the botanical family of Fagaceae (Beech). They are native to temperate areas of the Northern Hemisphere. Most are large trees that are very long-lived. They do best in dry soils and tolerate drought and shallow soils very well.

Chestnuts are used in this spell because they provide solid grounding energy while promoting longevity and boosting energy — perfect for regeneration to occur. If you are feeling zapped of strength, motivation and physical, mental or even emotional ability, then try these delicious chocolate chestnut magick truffles.

Timings

New Moon, Monday, Late Night

Find and Gather

- » 1 cup of plain sweet biscuits (*cookies*)
- » a large bowl
- » ⅓ cup of cocoa powder
- » a large, clean plastic food-grade bag
- » ½ cup of finely chopped Chestnuts (*Castanea sativa*)

Plate XL.—The Chestnut Tree of Mount Etna (*Castanea vulgaris*).

- » ¼ cup of desiccated coconut
- » a wooden spoon
- » 395-gram (*14-ounce*) can of condensed milk
- » a flat plate
- » ½ cup finely grated dark chocolate

The Spell

Place the biscuits (cookies) into the plastic bag and hit with a rolling pin to crush finely. Put these in the bowl along with the cocoa powder, desiccated coconut and chopped nuts. Slowly pour in the condensed milk while mixing with the wooden spoon, and say three times:

Chocolate treat,

Energy sweet,

Chestnut divine,

Strong energy mine.

Place in the fridge for ⅓ hour so that the mixture firms. Spread out the grated chocolate on to the flat plate. Roll tablespoons of the mixture into balls and then roll in the grated chocolate to coat.

These will keep in an airtight container in the fridge for up to four days. Eat one (or two!) when you need regenerating energies.

The Japanese eat Chestnuts on New Year's Day to ensure success and to give them the strength needed for the coming year. They are considered symbolic of difficulties and overcoming them in Japan.

Eating Chestnuts encourages fertility and carrying them will increase desire for you from others. Bowls of Chestnuts around the home are said to increase abundance for the household, but you must eat them.

Sequoia Tree Spell for Those in Need

All Sequoia trees (also known as redwoods) have very distinctive red fibrous bark and the species includes some of the oldest and tallest trees in the world. Many of the species are now extinct and have only been named after the discovery of their fossils. They are found in the Northern Hemisphere.

Not everyone will have access to a Sequoia tree for this spell, but you can find the tallest tree in your neighbourhood and still bring the energy of this mighty giant to you. Their power and majesty really can reach around the world! This spell is based loosely on the wish-granting Clootie Tree. In the UK, Ireland and particularly Cornwall these magickal trees are known by many names including May Bushes, Rag Trees and Faerie Trees.

Timings

Full Moon, Sunday, Night

Find and Gather

» a Sequoia tree (*Sequoia* spp.) or a proxy tree (*see page 12*)
» a pink ribbon, any length (*for healing*)
» a red ribbon, any length (*for strength*)
» a green ribbon, any length (*for new paths*)

The Spell

Sit on the ground with your back against the tree. Take some time to just sit and listen to the tree and get to know it. Talk to the tree, telling it who and what your request for help from the tree is all about. When you feel ready, take the three ribbons, stand before the tree and say:

For you, great Sequoia,
The ribbons of three,
I ask that you help,
Those I know in need.

Tie the pink ribbon on the tree (to a branch if possible) and say:

Pink is for healing,
Complete and true.

Take the red ribbon, tie it to the tree and say:

Red is for strength,
Courage and faith.

Tie the green ribbon to the tree and say:

And green for new growth,
For us and for you.

Giant Sequoias (*Sequoiadendron giganteum*), or Giant Redwoods, are the world's largest single trees and they usually grow to an average height of 50–85 metres (*164–279 feet*) and 6–8 metres (*20–26 feet*) in diameter. There have been trees recorded at 94.8 m (*311 feet*) in height.

It is believed that the giant Sequoias are a link between heaven and earth and can also draw power from the heavens. They are often used in magick that connects us with nature and with the divine.

Almond Tree Grief Support Spell

Almond trees are widely distributed throughout the world due to the popularity of their nuts (also called almond), which have been cultivated for over 2000 years. They are native to the Middle East, particularly Mediterranean climate regions.

This is a very gentle and soothing bath spell that you can create for yourself or another to support and comfort during times of grief. Almond tree is included as it has rejuvenation qualities and can help gently with any unresolved issues or feelings.

Timings

Full Moon, Sunday, Dusk

Find and Gather

» 2 white candles and holders

» matches

» 4 tablespoons of sweet Almond oil (*Prunus dulcis*)

» 2 tablespoons of sea salt

» 8 drops of Rose oil (*Rosa* spp.)

» a rose quartz crystal

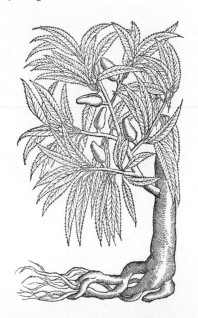

The Spell

Set the candles safely on, or very close to, your bath.

Light them and say:

White light of protection,

Surround in your grace.

Run your bath, add the sweet Almond oil and say:

Heal and glow.

Then add the sea salt, and say:

Ground and balance.

Add the Rose oil and say:

Love and protect.

Once the bath is filled to your liking, take your rose quartz crystal with you and immerse yourself in the healing and replenishing waters for as long as you like.

Carrying Almonds in your pockets is supposed to lead you to reassurance. Dreaming of eating them foretells that a journey is imminent and eating them will increase your wisdom. If you are looking for success in business, climb an Almond tree.

The almond shape is found repeated in medieval art, quite often surrounding God, Christ and the Virgin Mother. In Christianity the almond shape symbolises the intersection of the circles between heaven and earth.

Myrtle Tree Celebration Spell

Common Myrtle is native to the Mediterranean region in southern Europe, western Asia, Macaronesia, the Indian subcontinent and North Africa. There are many trees with 'Myrtle' in their name because they share similar characteristics but only one true Myrtle: Myrtus communis.

Group spells create amazing magick and are a perfect way to tap into the energies and make something long-lasting with all those present at a gathering. This spell can be done at any type of get-together but works well to channel the good will, joy and atmosphere of celebrations. Planting a tree is a time-honoured tradition at such times and the use of Myrtle will ensure longevity and love. Myrtle also has close associations with marriage and relationships, so this would also be the perfect engagement celebration spell.

Timings
Full Moon, Friday, Any Time

Find and Gather

» ribbons, each 1 metre (*40 inches*) long
» gardening tools
» a very small quartz crystal for each person
» a Myrtle plant (*M. communis*) – a cutting or sapling
» water

The Spell

Ask each guest to bring a ribbon to your celebration and have some extras on hand for those who might have forgotten. Dig the hole for the Myrtle. Have each person lay their ribbon with one end touching the hole and the rest stretched out flat on the ground, with a small quartz crystal at the other end. The ribbons should all fan out around the central hole like a sunburst. You can ask the guests to make a wish for the celebration or themselves or share something.

All stand around the starburst and if you can, hold hands and say:

Together we stand and energy raise,

The love and hope,

To last for all coming days.

You might like to edit this to suit your celebration or gathering.

Plant the Myrtle, water well.

Have each person take their ribbon and crystal home. This will contain the magick of the spell for them personally. If your gathering is a recurring event, they may like to bring the ribbon and crystal back with them. In the years that follow, cuttings from the Myrtle can be shared with those who were present as a way to continue the energy and hopes of the original day.

The Common Myrtle is one of the four species used by those observing the Jewish faith during the festival of Sukkot (*Feast of Tabernacles*). Celebrated on the fifteenth day of the seventh month, it marks the end of the harvest time in the Land of Israel.

Drinking Myrtle tea once every three days, or wearing Myrtle, is said to ensure you remain young-looking. This old folk tradition has been proven at least partly correct as it has been shown that certain Myrtles contain antioxidants that benefit the skin.

Acacia Tree Morning Ritual

There are over 1200 species of Acacia, with more than 900 of these being native to Australia, and they make up that country's largest flowering genus. They are also found in Africa. On both continents Acacias are found in all types of terrestrial habitats, from woodland, alpine and coastal dunes to rainforests, grasslands and deserts.

Wattleseed tea is a zingy botanical brew that will bring the energies of new beginnings, hope and joy to your day. It can be brewed alone in a coffee plunger, added to your regular coffee or tea as in this spell, or added to a warm glass of water with a slice of lemon. Dedicate a special cup or mug just for this ritual. Make sure it is brightly coloured.

Timings

Any Moon Phase, Any Day, Morning

Find and Gather

» Roasted ground wattleseed (*Acacia* spp.)

» your usual tea or coffee

» a special morning ritual cup or mug

» a journal

» a pen

The Spell

I have a journal that I keep everything in. It's overflowing with spells, sketches, shopping lists

and to-do lists as well as my daily journals. You might do this too or perhaps you have a special journal dedicated to your morning ritual. Have it ready in the place that you will take your coffee or tea. Set this time away from computers and phone, somewhere lovely.

Make your morning beverage and as you complete the task, say:

Today I awake,

To a day that is new,

Possibilities positive,

In all I may do.

In as jaunty manner as you can, throw in a dash of wattleseed and say:

Grow little suns,

Glow and shimmer with glee.

Bring a day that is bright,

And happy for me.

Grab your journal and drink. Sit in your lovely place and make some positive notes on what could unfold today. I have a dried Wattle leaf as my journal bookmark and I often find myself sketching a few Wattle flowers each morning, too. It all helps to bring their uplifting energies into my day.

The Acacia is a symbol of eternal life and of protection across many cultures. The final resting place of the god Osiris, lord of the Underworld, is said be an Acacia and this is why he is also known as 'lord of the Acacia'. The Freemasons use the Acacia as a symbol of eternal life.

Acacia is worn by Buddhists and Hindus, as the tree is considered sacred by them and is believed to offer them protection. Hindus sometimes wear a sprig in their turbans for this reason.

Sandalwood Evening Blessing Ritual

Sandalwood, also known as Indian Sandalwood, is a small tree native to India, Indonesia and the Malay Archipelago. The fragrance and medicinal qualities of the wood of this tree are important to many cultures and faiths.

Sandalwood helps clear negativity. It also sharpens mental focus onto what really matters and will help wishes come true – all good qualities for a night-time ritual. This spell creates a lightly fragrant balm that you can dab lightly on yourself before retiring for the night.

Timings
Full Moon, Saturday, Night

Find and Gather
» 2 tablespoons of vegetable wax
» a saucepan
» a heat-proof bowl
» 2 drops of Rose essential oil (*Rosa* spp.)
» a wooden spoon
» 2 drops of Sandalwood essential oil (*Santalum album*)
» 2 tablespoons of grapeseed oil
» a beautiful sterilised jar with a lid

The Spell

Carefully melt the wax over a low heat in the saucepan and then pour into the heat-proof bowl. Add the Rose oil and, stirring with the wooden spoon, say:

Sweetly cleanse away the day,

Of things that here,

Should really stay.

Calm so sweetly,

Calm so sweetly.

Add the Sandalwood oil and, stirring, say:

Negativity be gone and be done,

Tonight I lie softly,

Until tomorrow's new sun.

Pour into the warm jar and let cool. Once set, put the lid on and store in a cool, dry, dark place for up to six months. To use, dab a little on your pulse points.

According to folklore, wishes can be granted by Sandalwood. The best way is to write your wish on a piece of Sandalwood and then burn it. The smoke should rise and release, finding ways to grant your wish.

Sandalwood and Lavender (*Lavandula* spp.) together create a powerful spirit world connector. You could create a spell using both plants or you could replace the Rose oil in this spell with Lavender essential oil to make a balm that will help deepen your spirit communication experiences.

European Beech Ancient Wisdom Awakening Spell

The European Beech is the most dominant tree in the woodlands of southern Britain. It is also a popular street and park tree in temperate areas of the world, especially North America. The Beech is often clipped into a hedge.

This spell will increase your awareness while studying ancient wisdom and assist you to find ways to use it. European Beech not only helps open paths to wisdom, it imparts the energies of luck and success. By creating the bookmark in this spell, you will have a long-lasting guide and energy booster to carry with you as you study. Select your old book in a subject that you are passionate about as the wisdom within it will also carry into the bookmark.

Timings

Full Moon, Wednesday, Dusk

Find and Gather

- » 4–6 leaves of European Beech (*Fagus sylvatica*)
- » a large, heavy old book
- » a piece of cardboard – bookmark-sized to your preference
- » glue (*suitable for paper crafts*)
- » clear contact paper or wide, clear packing tape
- » scissors
- » paper towels

The Spell

Open your book and say:

> Old friend of wisdom,
>
> Keeper of power,
>
> Press my leaves of Beech,
>
> To help me also empower.

Place a paper towel on the page and lay your leaves out flat and spaced well so they are not touching each other. You can use more than one page if you need. Make sure you cover the leaves with an additional paper towel.

Close the book and add a few more heavy books on top so it is weighted down to press the leaves. Store in a cool, dry place for three weeks, then check on your leaves: if they are dried out then proceed; if not, leave for a while longer.

Place and glue the dried leaves as you desire on your cardboard bookmark, then cover neatly with contact or packing tape. Use in books when you study, in your journal or lean up against computers you are researching on.

There are many indications for the use of Beech in spellwork including sprinkling some ground Beech powder in your right shoe to lead you to success and fortune, carrying pieces in your pocket for luck and making wishes come true by burying pieces.

The botanical name for Beech comes to us from the Ancient Celts who resided in what is now France. They worshipped a god named Fagus, the god of babies and childbirth. Concoctions created from the Beech tree have been used as a disinfectant throughout Europe for hundreds of years.

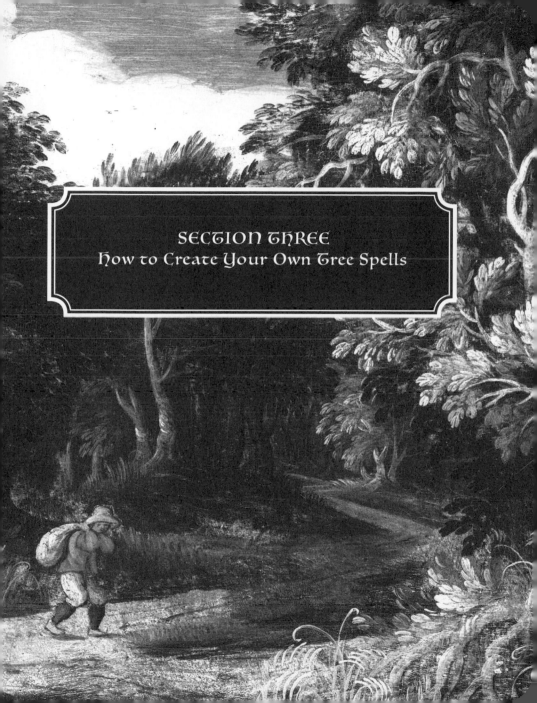

SECTION THREE
How to Create Your Own Tree Spells

Ḥow to Create Your Own Ḡree Spells

❦ TREES IN SPELLS

To use a tree in a spell you should understand its energy and to do this, you need to know its meaning and attributes. You can find these by exploring the properties it has or look to resources such as aromatherapy, herbal medicine guides and botanical history resources that discuss the properties of plants.

❦ MAGICKAL CORRESPONDENCES

You may wish to create a bath, essence, tea, mandala – anything at all that will be in itself an action related to the energy of the spell. Items required for this should be aligned with your outcome. These are usually called *Correspondences* or *Magickal Correspondences*. Expand your knowledge in areas that you do not have experience with by seeking out resources that specialise in the correspondence you wish to include, such as Astrological, Crystal, Colour and so on. Following is a brief list of such correspondences to get you started:

Colour

You can use colour in cloths to set your spell upon, in the tools that you use, candles and in the flowers themselves and in additional ingredients.

Red: passion, power, strength, courage, renewal, health, motivation, self-esteem, confrontation, ambition, challenge, purchases

Pink: healing, calming, emotions, harmony, compassion, self-love, romance, relaxation, new beginnings, partnerships

Orange: opportunities, legal matters, obstacles, abundance, gain, power, happiness

Yellow: friendship, returns, productivity, creativity, education, healing

Green: wellness, new beginnings, marriage, home, planning, peace, harmony, birth, rebirth, fertility, affection, luck, change, creativity, socialising

Blue: self-improvement, opportunity, charity, study, growth, travel, insight, patience, meditation, sports, religion, social standing, expansion, higher education, wisdom

Brown: focus, lost items, grounding, harvest, security, generosity, endurance

Violet: psychic growth, divination, spiritual development, self-improvement

Purple: spirit, ambition, protection, healing, intuition, business, occultism

White: protection, safety, protection, transformation, enlightenment, connection to higher self, becoming more outgoing, relieving shyness, the cycle of life, freedom, health, initiation

Black: divination, rebirth, material gain, discoveries, truth, sacrifice, protection, creation, death, karma, absorbing energies, binding, neutralising, debts, separation.

Timings

These are the times that you put spells together and when they are cast. They add an energetic boost to your spells by bringing alignment to what you are doing in the space you are creating it. I'm sharing simple ones here for you but you can also explore deeper seasonal timings, ones associated with traditional

Pagan celebrations and observances and ones that are unique to the area and people of where you live and are open to others.

Moon Phases

Waxing: new projects, beginnings, growth
Full: empowerment, healing, attainment
Waning: banishing, cleansing, letting go
New: divination, revelations

Day of the Week

Monday: home, family, dreams, emotions, female energies, gardens, medicine, psychic development, travel

Tuesday: courage, strength, politics, conflict, lust, endurance, competition, surgical procedures, sports, masculine energies

Wednesday: communication, divination, self-improvement, teaching, inspiration, study, learning

Thursday: luck, finances, legal matters, desires, honour, accomplishments, prosperity, material gain

Friday: friendship, pleasure, art, music, social activities, comfort, sensuality, romance

Saturday: life, protection, self-discipline, freedom, wisdom, goals, re-incarnation

Sunday: spirituality, power, healing, individuality, hope, healing, professional success, business

Time of Day

Dawn: beginnings, awakening, cleansing, new ideas, change, love
Morning: growth, home, gardening, finances, harmony, generosity
Midday: health, willpower physical energy, intellect

Afternoon: communication, business, clarity

Dusk/Twilight: reduction, change, receptiveness

Night: pleasure, joy, socialising, gatherings, play

Midnight: endings, release, recuperation

Crystals

The addition of crystals in the form of whole pieces, tumble stones, balls and jewellery can add the energies of each to your spell. Not all crystals are suitable for all types of spells as some are not safe when coming in contact with items you use for consumption or topically.

You will need to check these as you create your spells with a reliable specialised crystal usage resource.

Agate: courage, longevity, love, protection, healing, self-confidence

Agate, Black: success, courage

Agate, Black and White: physical protection

Agate, Blue Lace: peace, consciousness, trust, self-expression

Agate, Green Moss: healing, longevity, gardening, harmony, abundance

Amazonite: creativity, unity, success, thought process

Amber: protection, luck, health, calming, humour, spell breaker, manifestation

Amethyst: peace, love, protection, courage, happiness, psychic protection

Apache Tear: protection from negative energy, grief, danger, forgiveness

Apatite: control, communication, coordination

Aquamarine: calm, strength, control, fears, tension relief, thought processes

Aventurine: independence, money, career, sight, intellect, sport, leadership

Azurite: divination, healing, illusions, communication, psychic development

Bloodstone: healing, business, strength, power, legal matters, obstacles

Calcite: purification, money, energy, spiritualty, happiness

Carnelian: courage, sexual energy, fear, sorrow release, action, motivation

Chalcedony: emotions, honesty, optimism

Chrysocolla: creativity, female energies, communication, wisdom

Citrine: detox, abundance, regeneration, cleansing, clarity, initiative

Dioptase: love attracter, prosperity, health, relaxation

Emerald: wealth, protection, intellect, artistic talent, tranquillity, memory

Epidote: emotional healing, spirituality

Fluorite: study, intellect, comprehension, balance, concentration

Garnet: protection, strength, movement, confidence, devotion

Gold: power, success. healing, purification, honour, masculine energy

Hematite: divination, common sense, grounding, reasoning, relationships

Herkimer Diamond: tension soothing, sleep, rest, power booster

Iolite: soul connection, visions, discord release

Jade: justice, wisdom, courage, modesty, charity, dreams, harmony

Jasper: healing, health, beauty, nurturing, travel

Jet: finances, anti-nightmares, divination, health, luck, calms fears

Kunzite: addiction, maturity, security, divinity

Kyanite: dreams, creativity, vocalization, clarity, serenity, channelling

Labradorite: destiny, elements

Lapis Lazuli: love, fidelity, joy, healing, psychic development, inner truth

Larimar: confidence, depression, serenity, energy balance

Malachite: money, sleep, travel, protection, business

Moldavite: changes, transformation, life purpose

Moonstone: youth, habits, divination, love, protection, friends

Obsidian: grounding, production, peace, divination

Onyx: stress, grief, marriage, nightmare protection, self-control

Opal: beauty, luck, power, money, astral projection

Pearl: faith, integrity, innocence, sincerity, luck, money, love

Peridot: wealth, stress, fear, guilt, personal growth, health

Prehnite: chakras, relationships

Pyrite: memory, focus, divination, luck

Quartz, Clear: protection, healing, power, psychic power

Quartz, Rose: love, peace, happiness, companionship

Quartz, Smokey: depression, negativity, tension, purification

Rhodochrosite: new love, peace, energy, mental powers, trauma healing

Ruby: wealth, mental balance, joy, power, contentment, intuition

Sapphire: meditation, protection, power, love, money, wisdom, hope

Sardonyx: progression, finances, self-protection

Selenite: decisions, reconciliation, flexibility, clarity

Silver: stress, travel, invocation, dreams, peace, protection, energy

Sodalite: wisdom, prophetic dreams, dissipates confusion

Sugilite: physical healing, heart, wisdom, spirituality

Sunstone: sexual healing, energy, protection, health

Tanzanite: magick, insight, awareness

Tiger's Eye: courage, money, protection, divination, energy, luck

Topaz: love, money, sleep, prosperity, commitment, calm

Tourmaline: friendship, business, health, astral projection

Tourmaline, Black: grounding, protection,

Tourmaline, Blue: peace, stress relief, clear speech

Tourmaline, Green: success, creativity, goals, connection with nature

Tourmaline, Pink: friendship, love, creativity

Tourmaline, Red: projection, courage, energy

Turquoise: protection, communication, socialising, health, creative solutions

❧ FLOWER MEANINGS

Of course, most trees have flowers and you can also use floral references that will explore meanings and uses to develop your own spells. Flowers hold the same energy as the rest of the plant. In fact, they give a little additional boost to that energy as the plant is in the process of reproduction.

These are just some of the flowers that you can find in my book *Flowerpaedia: 1000 Flowers and Their Meanings* (Cheralyn Darcey, Rockpool Publishing, Sydney, Australia, 2017). Some of them are also used in the spells in this book.

Agrimony *(Agrimonia eupatoria):* do not worry, inner fears and worries

Allspice *(Pimenta dioica):* you are worthy, self-value, self-nurture

Angelica *(Angelica archangelica)*: inspiration, spiritual protection, facing the unknown, protection

Basil *(Ocimum basilicum)*: travel well, open heart, compassion, strengthen faith, spirituality, peace, love, fidelity, virtue, preservation, mourning, courage in difficulties, harmony

Burdock *(Arctium)*: do not touch me, protection, healing, persistence, importunity, core issues, release anger

Catnip *(Nepeta cataria)*: calm hysteria, clarity, focus, female healing

Chamomile, German *(Matricaria chamomilla)*: equilibrium, relax, calm down, release tension, soothing, ease nightmares, energy, patience in adversity, nervous system support, love, attract love

Chamomile, Roman: (Chamaemelum nobile): I admire your courage, do not despair, love in austerity, patience, abundance, attract wealth, fortitude, calm

Chicory *(Cichorium intybus)*: I love you unconditionally, removal of obstacles, invisibility, momentum, release of tension, favours, frigidity, unconditional love

Chives *(Allium schoenoprasum)*: protection from evil spirits, protection of house, weight loss, protection, long life

Cinnamon *(Cinnamomum verum)*: forgiveness of hurt, clairvoyance, creativity, defence, divination, dreams, healing, love, mediation, psychic development, purification, spirituality, success, wealth, power

Cloves *(Eugenia caryophyllata)*: protection, dignity, exorcism, love, money

Coltsfoot *(Tussilago farfara)*: I am concerned for you, maternal love, concern, children, new challenges, vitality, physical stamina, immunity

Comfrey *(Symphytum officinale)*: healing, fusion

Dandelion *(Taraxacum officinale)*: I am faithful to you, your wish is granted, long-lasting happiness, healing, intelligence, warmth, power, clarity, survival

Dill *(Anethum graveolens)*: lust, luck, protection from evil, finances

Echinacea *(Echinacea purpurea)*: higher self, strength, physical strength, immunity, healing, dignity, wholeness, integrity

Foxglove *(Digitalis purpurea)*: I believe in you, beware, stateliness, communication, insincerity, magic, confidence, creativity, youth

Frankincense *(Boswellia sacra)*: faithful heart, blessing, consecration, courage, divination, energy, exorcism, love, luck, meditation, power, protection, purification, spiritual growth, spirituality, strength, success, visions

Gardenia *(Gardenia jasminoides)*: awareness, secret love, divine message

Garlic *(Allium sativum)*: good fortune, protection, strength, courage, aphrodisiac, wholeness, immunity

Ginger *(Zingiber officinale)*: you are loved, clarity, determination, intelligence, courage, warm feelings, tension relief, sensitivity, perception, sensory awareness

Ginkgo *(Gingko biloba)*: beauty, business, calling spirits, dreams, fertility, longevity, love

Ginseng *(Panax spp.)*: love, wishes, beauty, protection, lust, grounding, balance, disconnection, longevity, mental powers

Goldenseal *(Hydrastis canadensis)*: healing, money

Gotu Kola *(Hydrocotyle asiatica)*: self-awareness

Guarana *(Paullinia cupana)*: wishes, energy

Hawthorn *(Crataegus monogyna)*: balance, duality, purification, sacred union, hope, heart protection

Honeysuckle *(Lonicera spp.)*: Be happy, I am devoted to you, happiness, sweet disposition, sweet life, end arguments, homesickness, intimacy, unity

Hop *(Humulus lupulus)*: apathy, injustice, passion, pride, healing, sleep, mirth

Hyssop *(Hyssopus officinalis)*: I forgive you, cleanliness, sacrifice, breath, forgiveness, purification, shame, guilt, pardon, repentance

Juniper *(Juniperus spp.)*: journey, protection, anti-theft, love, exorcism, health, healing, cleansing, purifying spaces

Laurel *(Laurus nobilis)*: I change but in death, I admire you but cannot love you, victory, protection from disease, protection from witchcraft, merit, glory

Lavender *(Lavendula stoechas)*: cleansing, protection, grace, trust, I admire you

Lemon Balm *(Melissa officinalis)*: lift spirits, renewed youth, calm, strengthen mind, restore health, vigour, balance emotions, relax, courage, inner strength

Lemon Verbena *(Aloysia triphylla)*: attractiveness, love, protection from nightmares, sweet dreams, marriage, purification

Lemongrass *(Cymbopogon citratus)*: friendship, lust, psychic awareness, purification, protection from snakes

Marshmallow *(Althea officinalis)*: to cure, humanity, dispel evil spirits, attract good spirits, beneficence, mother, maternal energies, protection

Meadowsweet *(Filipendula ulmaria)*: healing, love, divination, peace, happiness, protection from evil, balance, harmony

Motherwort *(Leonurus cardiaca)*: concealed love, female healing, inner trust, spiritual healing, astral travel, immortality, longevity, relationship balance, mothering issues, sedation, calm anxiety

Mugwort *(Artemisia vulgaris)*: prophecy, protection, strength, psychic abilities, prophetic dreams, healing, astral projection, awkwardness, creative visualisation, visions, clairvoyance, divination

Nettle *(Urtica spp.)*: you are cruel, you are spiteful, cruelty, pain, slander, clear choices, decision making, protection against evil spirits, health recovery

Onion *(Allium cepa)*: protection, purification, detox, hibernating energy, potential

Oregano *(Origanum vulgare)*: joy, happiness, honour

Parsley *(Petroselinum crispum)*: entertainment, fest, protection of food, festivity, to win, useful knowledge

Passion Flower *(Passiflora incarnate)*: I am pledged to another, belief, passion, religious superstition, religious work, stability, spiritual balance, higher consciousness

Patchouli *(Pogostemon cablin)*: defence, fertility, releasing, love, wealth, sexual power

Peppermint *(Mentha piperita)*: friendship, love, clarity, refreshment, concentration, clear thinking, inspiration, energy, alert mind, study support

Scottish Primrose *(Primula scotica)*: I love you completely, I'm sorry, compassion, acceptance, anxiety, forgiveness, unconditional love, patience

Red Clover *(Trifolium pratense)*: good fortune, good luck, fertility, domestic virtue, protection from danger, psychic protection, cleansing, clear negativity, balance, calmness, clarity, enhance self-awareness

Rosemary *(Rosmarinus officinalis)*: I remember you, your presence revives me, psychic awareness, mental strength, accuracy, clarity, remembrance, memory

Sage *(Salvia officinalis)*: purification, longevity, good health, long life, wisdom, cleansing, protection, higher purpose, reflection, inner peace, esteem, domestic virtue

Sandalwood *(Santalum album)*: clear negativity, mental focus, reincarnation, wishes

Skullcap *(Scutellaria* spp.*)*: relaxation, psychic healing, relaxation of nerves, self-esteem, ability to cope

Slippery Elm *(Ulmus rubra)*: stop gossip

Sweet Marjoram *(Origanum marjorana)*: let go of fear, self-reliance, comforting, relieve physical tension, relieve mental tension, consolation, protection from lightning, comfort grief, fertility, love, joy, honour, good fortune, long life

Thyme *(Thymus vulgaris)*: bravery, affection, courage, strength, let's do something, activity

Wormwood *(Artemisia absinthium)*: do not be discouraged, absence, authenticity, sorrowful parting

Yarrow *(Achillea millefolium)*: friendship, war, elegance, banishing, relaxation

Flowerpaedia can also be used to look up energies and themes and so find flowers, herbs and plants that you wish to include in your spell. Following is a small sample from the book:

Change: Bee Balm *(Monarda* spp.*)*, Scarlet Pimpernel *(Anagalis arvensis),* Mayflower *(Epigaea repens),* Fireweed *(Chamerion angustifolium),* Snowplant *(Sarcodes sanquinea)*

Clarity: Boronia *(Boronia ledifolia),* Grass Tree *(Xanthorrhoea resinosa),* Sweet Alyssum *(Alyssum maritimum),* Hemp *(Cannabis Sativa),* Angel's Trumpet *(Brugmansia candida),* Dandelion *(Taraxacum officinale),* Petunia *(Petunia),* Hippeastrum *(Hippeastrum),* Rosemary *(Rosmarinus officinalis),* Trout Lily *(Erythronium americanum),* Greater Celandine *(Chelidonium majus),* Peppermint *(Mentha piperita),* Catnip *(Nepeta cataria),* Clary Sage *(Salvia sclarea),* Red Clover *(Trifolium pretense),* Ginger *(Zingiber officinale),* Carrot *(Daucus carota* subsp. *sativus),* Grapefruit *(Citrus parasisi),* Coffee *(Coffea arabica)*

Clarity, emotional: Love-in-a-Mist *(Nigella damascene),* Gerbera Daisy, Yellow *(Gerbera jamesonii)*

Deceit: Mock Orange *(Philadelphus),* Venus Flytrap *(Dionaea muscipula),* Lewis Mock Orange *(Philadelphus lewisii),* Dogbane *(Apocynum cannabinum),* Fly Orchid *(Ophrys insectifera),* Rocket *(Eruca sativa)*

Encouragement: Madonna Lily *(Lilium candidum),* Carnation, Pink *(Dianthus caryophyllus),* Dahlia *(Dahlia* spp.*),* Goldenrod *(Solidago virgaurea),* Black-Eyed Susan *(Rudbeckia hirta),* Campion, red *(Silene),* Bayberry *(Myrica),* Watermelon *(Citrullus lanatus),* Butterfly Lily *(Hedychium coronarium)*

Release: Lechenaultia *(Lechenaultia formas),* Henbane *(Hyoscyamus niger),* Calendula *(Calendula officinalis),* Skunk Cabbage *(Symplocarpus foetidus),* Alder *(Alnus),* Rose, Meadow *(Rosa blanda),* Butterfly Weed *(Asclepias tuberosa),* Moneywort *(Bacopa monnieri),* Melilot *(Melilotus officinalis),* Air Plant *(Tillandsia* spp.*)*

Release anger: Burdock *(Arctium* spp.*),* Firethorn *(Pyracantha* spp.*)*

Release attachments: Trumpet Creeper *(Campisis radicans)*

Release barriers: Lady's Mantle *(Alchemilla vulgaris)*

Survival: Waratah *(Telopea speciosissima)*, Dandelion *(Taraxacum officinale)*, Tropic bird Orchid *(Angraecum eburneum)*, Texas Bluebonnet *(Lupinus texensis)*, Kapok *(Bomliax ceilia)*

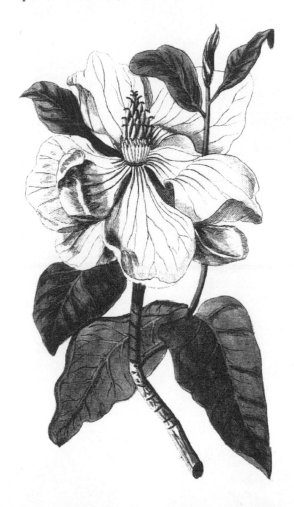

YOUR TREE SPELL
JOURNAL

Title

....

Description

....
....
....

Find and Gather

....
....
....

The Spell

....
....
....
....
....
....
....
....
....

Title

....

Description

....

....

....

Find and Gather

....

....

....

The Spell

....

....

....

....

....

....

....

....

Title

....

Description

....

....

....

Find and Gather

....

....

....

The Spell

....

....

....

....

....

....

....

....

Title

....

Description

....

....

....

Find and Gather

....

....

....

The Spell

....

....

....

....

....

....

....

....

Title

....

Description

....

....

....

Find and Gather

....

....

....

The Spell

....

....

....

....

....

....

....

....

Title

....

Description

....

....

....

Find and Gather

....

....

....

The Spell

....

....

....

....

....

....

....

....

Title

....

Description

....

....

....

Find and Gather

....

....

....

The Spell

....

....

....

....

....

....

....

....

Title

....

Description

....

....

....

Find and Gather

....

....

....

The Spell

....

....

....

....

....

....

....

....

Glossary of Magickal and Botanical Terms

apothecary: a storehouse or shop containing magickal supplies.

basal: arising from the root crown of a plant.

bulb: underground stem with modified leaves that contain stored food for plant shoot within.

bract: a modified leaf which sometimes looks like a petal.

bracteole: leaf-like projections.

cardinal points: directions on a compass.

cast: to create and release magick.

corm: the underground bulb-like part of some plants.

corona: a ring of structures which rise like a tube from a flower.

compound leaf: a leaf with a division of its form of two or more small leaf-like structures.

cultivar: a plant that has agricultural or horticultural use and whose unique characteristics are reproduced during propagation.

cut flower: a flower used as decoration.

dominant hand: the hand you are more proficient with.

endemic: native or restricted to a certain place.

flower head: a compact mass of flowers forming what appears to be a single flower.

floret: one of the small flowers making up a flower head.

Full Moon: when the moon is fully visible as a round disk.

genus: a botanical classification term that refers to a group smaller than a family but larger than a species.

grounded: to be fully connected with your physical being and the Earth.

grounding: to bring yourself back into the everyday world.

hermaphrodite: having both male and female reproductive parts.

hermaphrodic: having both male and female reproductive parts.

hex: a spell cast to cause harm.

inflorescence: several flowers closely grouped together to form one unit or the particular arrangement of flowers on a plant.

lobe: a rounded or projected part.

lanceolate: shaped like a lance, tapering at a point at each end.

leaflet: a small leaf or leaf-like part or part of a compound leaf.

leguminous: an erect or climbing bean or pea plant.

magick: metaphysical work to bring about change.

mojo bag: a magic into which magickal items are placed and usually worn on the person

New Moon: the moon phase when the moon is not visible.

oracle: a person who translates divination messages between the Other Worlds and people.

ovate: egg shaped with a broader end at the base.

Pagan: originally meaning people who lived in the countryside and now meaning those who follow nature-based spirituality and hold beliefs other than the main religions of the world.

panicle: a loose cluster of flowers on a branch.

parasitic: gains all or part of its nutritional needs from another living plant.

perennial: a plant which lives for three or more years.

pericarpel: the cup like structure of a flower on which the sepals, petals and stamens sit.

pinnate: feather like.

pollarding: pruning a tree of the upper branches to promote a dense head of foliage and branches.

pseudanthium: a flower head consisting of many tiny flowers.

raceme: inflorescence in which the main axis produces a series of flowers on lateral stalks.

ray flower: a flower which resembles a petal.

ritual: a ceremony which combines actions and sometimes words, music

sessile: attached without a stalk.

stamen: the pollen producing reproductive organ of a flower.

staminal column: a structure, in column form containing the male reproductive organ of plant.

scrying: using a reflective surface or a body of water in divination to gaze into.

steep: to leave in hot water so that properties are imparted via heat into the water.

stem: the main part of a plant, usually rising above the ground

spent: flowers or plants which are dead.

tepal: a segment in a flower that has no differentiation between petals and sepals.

thermogenic: the ability to generate own heat and maintain it.

tuber: a thickened part of an underground stem

Vodoun: a religion created by African ethnic groups in colonial Saint-Domingue and then blended with Christianity in the 16th and 17th centuries.

Waxing Moon: the moon is getting larger, towards full.

Waning Moon: the moon is getting smaller, towards dark/new.

Witch Bottle: a bottle filled with items then sealed and usually buried to create a spell.

Bibliography

Coombes, Allen J. *Dictionary of Plant Names* (Timber Press 2002)

Cunningham, Scott, *Encyclopedia of Magical Herbs* (Llewellyn Publications 2010)

Graves, Julia, *The Language of Plants* (Lindisfarne Books 2012)

Hanson, J. Wesley, *Flora's Dial* (Jonathan Allen 1846)

Harrison, Lorraine, *RHS Latin for Gardeners* (Mitchell Beazley 2012)

Hemphill, John & Rosemary, *Myths and Legends of the Garden* (Hodder & Stoughton 1997)

Hill, Lewis and Hill, Nancy, *The Flower Gardener's Bible* (Storey Publishing 2003)

Kelly, Frances, *The Illustrated Language of Flowers* (Viking O'Neil 1992)

Macboy, Stirling *What Flower Is That?* (Lansdowne Press 2000)

Olds, Margaret, *Flora's Plant Names* (Gordon Cheers 2003)

Pavord, Anna *The Naming of Names: The Search for Order in the World of Plants* (Bloomsbury 2005)

Phillips, Stuart, *An Encyclopaedia of Plants in Myth, Legend, Magic and Lore* (Robert Hale Limited 2012)

Thomsen, Michael and Gennat, Hanni, *Phyotherapy Desk Reference* (Global Natural Medicine 2009)

Vickery, Roy, *A Dictionary of Plant-Lore* (Oxford University Press 1995)

Image Credits

Introduction
   In the City of Flowers, Marshall, Emma (Seeley & Co., London 1889)
How to Use This Book
   The White Witch, Warden, Florence (Richard Bentley & Son, London 1884)
SECTION ONE
   Peasants on a path in a forest, Lanen, J. van der (1626)
What Is a Spell and How Does It Work?
   The History of Springfield in Massachusetts, Barrows, Charles H. (The Connecticut Valley Historical Society, Springfield, Mass., 1921)
How to Create and Cast a Spell
   Algemeene Geschiedenis Der Wereld, Polak, Mozes S. (Amsterdam, 1841)
Working Magickally with Trees
   Discoveries in Australia, Stokes, John Lort (London, 1846)
Ingredients and Tools for Tree Spells
   Rookwood: A Romance, Ainsworth, William Harrison (London, 1881)
SECTION TWO:
A Collection of Tree Spells
   Scharf, Sir George K.C.B. & Tozer, Henry Fanshawe (John Murray, London, 1882)
Tree Spells for Balance and Harmony
   Master Wilberforce, A Study of a Boy 'Rita' (Hutchinson & Co., London, 1895)

Maple Tree Positive Energy Spell
  Pictorial Half-hours, Ed: Knight, Charles (Charles Knight, London, 1850)

Cedar Tree Gain Control Spell
  A History of British Forest-Trees, Indigenous and Introduced, Selby, Prideaux John (John van Voorst, London, 1842)

Lemon Tree Inspire Joy Spell
  Indian Medicinal Plants, Kirtikar, K.R., Basu, B.D. & I.C.S. (India, 1918)

Bodhi Tree Healing Spell
  Ceylon, Tennent, Sir James Emerson (Longman, Green, Longman & Roberts, London, 1860)

Blackthorn Tree Remove Negativity Spell
  Prose and Verse, Linton, William James (1836)

Holly Tree Find Balance Spell
  Scottish Rivers, Lauder, Sir Thomas Dick (Edinburgh, 1874)

Linden Tree Remove Stress Spell
  The Vegetable World: Being a History of Plants, Figuier, Louis. Ill: Faguet, M. (Chapman & Hall, London, 1867)

Rowan Tree Energy Protection Spell
  Revue Horticole, (Paris, 1829)

English Oak Tree Inner Strength Spell
  A School History of the United States, Swinton, William (American Book Co. New York, 1893)

Elm Tree Psychic Attack Shield Protection
  The Popular History of England, Knight, Charles (London, 1856)

Tree Spells for Modern Problems
  The United States of America, Shaler, Nathaniel Southgate (Sampson Low & Marston, London, 1894)

Larch Tree Social Media Protection Spell
  Ellwanger & Barry's Descriptive Catalogue of Ornamental Trees and Shrubs, Roses, Flowering Plants, Etc., Etc., Etc., (Ellwanger & Barry, Rochester, N.Y., 1868)

Alder Tree Dispute Shield Spell
  Stirpium Historiae Pemptades Sex: Sive Libri XXX, Dodonaeus (Dodoens), R. (1583)

Hazel Tree Study Spell
Hortus floridus: Fasicle Pars Altera, Passe, C. van de (1614)

Baobab Tree Traveller Spell
Die Pflanzenwelt Ost-Afrikas und der Nachbargebiete, Vol. 1, Engler, A. (1895)

Coconut Palm Tree Relaxation Spell
Der Fruchtbringenden Gesellschaft, Merian, M. (1646)

Jacaranda Tree Luck Money Spell
Curtis's Botanical Magazine, Vol. 128, (London, New York 1902)

White Mulberry Tree Wholeness Spell
Picturesque Palestine, Sinai and Egypt, Vol. 1, Wilson, C. (1881)

Eucalyptus Tree Stop Me Texting Spell
The World Before the Deluge, Figuier, Guillaume Louis (London, 1867)

Coral Tree Job Hunting Spell
Natal Plants, Vol. 4, Wood, J.M. & Evans, M.S. (1906)

Walnut Entrepreneur Spell
The Garden: An Illustrated Weekly Journal of Gardening in All Its Branches, Ed: William Robinson (London, 1871)

Tree Spells for Relationships and Love
Poems by Robert Burns: With an Account of His Life, Burns, Robert & contributor Walker, Josiah A.M. (Trustees of the late James Morison, Edinburgh, 1811)

Myrrh Tree Divorce Ritual
Joachimi Camerarii Symbolorum, Camerarius, Joachim (Mogvntiae, sumpt. L. Bovrgeat, typ. C. Kuchleri, 1668)

Flowering Dogwood Tree Boundary Spell
Songs for Little People, Gale, Norman Rowland. Ill: Stratton, Helen (Constable & Co., London, 1896)

Italian Cypress Tree Peaceful Separation Spell
The Garden. An Illustrated Weekly Journal of Horticulture in All Its Branches, Ed: William Robinson (London, 1871)

Pear Tree Regain Harmony Spell
Der Fruchtbringenden Gesellschaft, Merian, M. (1646)

White Willow Tree Healing Heartbreak Spell

The Vegetable World: Being a History of Plants, Figuier, Louis. Ill: Faguet, M. (Chapman & Hall, London, 1867)

Cherry Tree Love Reality Check Spell

Plantarum seu Stirpium Icones, Vol. 2, Lobel, M. de (1581)

Linden Tree Forgiveness Spell

Der Fruchtbringenden Gesellschaft, Merian, M.

Hawthorn Tree Strengthen Love Spell

La Belgique Horticole: Journal des Jardins et des Vergers, Vol. 1, (1851)

Apple Tree Love Spell

Florilegium, Das ist ein Blumenbuch, Völler [Voeller] von Gellhausen, U. (1616)

Sweet Orange Tree Friendship Spell

Tacuinum Sanitates, Halaf Ibn-Abbas Zahrawi (1380–1399)

Tree Spells for Change and Empowerment

L'Espace Céleste et la Nature Tropicale, Description Physique de L'univers, Liais, Emmanuel (Paris, 1866)

Eastern Cottonwood Tree Communication Spell

Revue Horticole, Serié 4, [3], Vol. 26, (1854)

Bay Laurel Tree Success Spell

Stirpium Historiae Pemptades Sex: Sive Libri XXX, R. Dodonaeus [Dodoens] (1583)

Magnolia Tree Legacy Protection Spell

Dreyhundert Auserlesene Amerikanische Gewächse, Vol. 2, Zorn, J., Jacquin, N.J.F. von (1786)

Spindle Tree Shadow Self Spell

Stirpium Historiae Pemptades Sex: Sive Libri XXX, Dodonaeus [Dodoens], R. (1583)

White Poplar Tree Guidance Spell

The Vegetable World: Being a History of Plants, Figuier, Louis. Ill: Faguet, M. (Chapman & Hall, London, 1867)

Dragon's Blood Tree Hex Breaker Spell

Botany of Socotra, Balfour, I.B. (Cockburn, 1888)

Mangrove Tree Opportunity Spell

MPI, Tissot, Victor & Constant, Améro (Paris, 1884)

Elder Tree Evolution Spell
Plantarum seu Stirpium Icones, Vol. 2, Lobel, M. de (1581)

Pine Tree Increase Intuition Spell
Reports of explorations and surveys, to ascertain the most practicable and economical route for a railroad from the Mississippi River to the Pacific Ocean in 1853–6, Vol. 6, Torrey, J. (1856)

Ash Tree Magickal Empowerment Spell
Der Wald, Rossmässler, E.A. Ill: Heyn, E. (1881)

Tree Spells for Purpose and Paths
The Poets Corner, or Haunts and Homes of the Poets, Corkran, Alice (Ernest Nister, E.P. Dutton & Co, London, 1892)

Spruce Tree Awaken My Passion Spell
Gartenflora, Regel, E. von (1888)

Hickory Tree Personal Path Spell
A Guide to the Trees, Lounsberry, A. Ill: Rowan, Ellis (1900)

Yew Tree Rebirth Spell
The Garden: An Illustrated Weekly Journal of Gardening in All Its Branches, Vol. 11, Ed: William Robinson (London, 1877)

Mesquite Tree Awaken Creativity Spell
Flora Indica, Burman, N.L. Ill: van der Laan, A. (1768)

Aspen Tree Overcome Obstacles Spell
Plantarum seu Stirpium Icones, Vol. 2, Lobel, M. de (1581)

Silver Fir Progress Spell
Der Wald, Rossmässler, E.A. Ill: Heyn, E. (1881)

Fig Tree Magickal Power Booster Spell
Plantarum seu Stirpium Icones, Vol. 2, Lobel, M. de (1581)

Silver Birch Tree Find Your Way Spell
Der Wald, Rossmässler, E.A. Ill: Heyn, E. (1881)

Hemlock Tree Secret Reveal Spell
Birds of America, Audubon, J.J. (J.J. Audubon, 1834)

Olive Tree Inner Peace Spell
Hortus floridus, Passe, C. van de (1614)

Tree Spells for the Earth and Life
> *Picturesque Scotland*, Watt, Francis & Carter, Andrew (J. Sangster & Co., London, 1887)

A Tree Planting Spell
> *Bountiful Ridge Nurseries*, Henry G. Gilbert Nursery & Seed Trade Catalog Collection (Princess Anne, MD, Bountiful Ridge Nurseries, 1948)

American Sycamore Gardener Success Spell
> *The Parent's Assistant*, Edgeworth, Maria (Macmillan & Co., London, 1897)

Palo Santo Tree Sacred Space Spell
> *The Mythology of All Races: Celtic and Slavic*, Gray, Louis Herbert; Moore, George Foot & MacCulloch, John Arnott (Marshall Jones Company, Boston, 1918)

Chestnut Tree Nature Regeneration Spell
> *The Vegetable World: Being a History of Plants*, Figuier, Louis. Ill: Faguet, M. (Chapman & Hall, London, 1867)

Sequoia Tree Spell for Those in Need
> *Narrative of the United States Exploring Expedition*, Wilkes, C. (1849)

Almond Tree Grief Support Spell
> *Stirpium historiae pemptades sex: sive libri XXX*, R. Dodonaeus [Dodoens] (1583)

Myrtle Tree Celebration Spell
> *Naauwkeurige Beschrijving der Aardgewassen*, Munting, A. (1696)

Acacia Tree Morning Ritual
> *Naauwkeurige Beschrijving der Aardgewassen, Vol. 1*, Munting, A. (1696)

Sandalwood Evening Blessing Ritual
> *Herbarium Amboinense, Vol. 2*, Rumphius, G.E. (1741)

European Beech Ancient Wisdom Awakening Spell
> *Der Wald*, Rossmässler, E.A. Ill: Heyn, E. (1881)

SECTION THREE: How to Create Your Own Tree Spells
> *The Garden*, Ed: William Robinson (London, 1876)

Your Tree Spell Journal
> *Life's Roses: A Volume of Selected Poems*, (E. Nister, London, 1898)

About the Author

Cheralyn Darcey is a botanical explorer, florist, organic gardener, environmental artist and the author and illustrator of over a dozen botanical titles. Through her books, she shares with readers her passion for nature and researching plants and their relationships with us. Living on the Central Coast of NSW, Australia, Cheralyn has created and nurtures her own extensive flower, vegetable and interesting plant home garden that has been featured in national publications and her creative sanctuary.

For more information, visit www.cheralyndarcey.com
Instagram: cheralyn
Youtube: Florasphere
Facebook: cheralyn.darcey

Other books by Cheralyn ...

The Book of Flower Spells

Beautiful to behold and sacred throughout time, flowers hold powerful nature magick, entwined with the rhythms of the Earth.

The Book of Herb Spells

Herbs can heal, comfort and nourish us with ancient energies used throughout time to create magickal spells.

The Book of Faerie Spells

Endless possibilities will open as you create your own divine spells to enrich your life under the Faeries' gracious and loving guidance.

Available from all good bookstores or online at
www.rockpoolpublishing.com.au